Incongruities

Who We Are and How We Pray

Edited by Timothy Fitzgerald and David A. Lysik

LITURGY
TRAINING
PUBLICATIONS

Acknowledgments

This book was edited by David A. Lysik. The production editor was Marie McLaughlin. The cover design and the typesetting in Sabon and Gill Sans were done by Anne Fritzinger. The interior design was done by Jill Smith. This book was printed by Webcom in Toronto, Canada. Cover images copyright © 1997 PhotoDisc, Inc.

INCONGRUITIES: WHO WE ARE AND HOW WE PRAY © 2000 Archdiocese of Chicago: Liturgy Training Publications, 1800 North Hermitage Avenue, Chicago IL 60622-1101; 1-800-933-1800; orders@ltp.org; fax 1-800-933-7094. All rights reserved.

Library of Congress Cataloging-in-publication Data
Incongruities: who we are and how we pray/edited by Timothy
   Fitzgerald and David A. Lysik.
      p. cm.
   Papers from the 27th Annual Conference of the Notre Dame
Center for Pastoral Liturgy, June 1999.
    ISBN 1-56854-355-7
    1. Lord's Supper—Catholic Church—Congresses.
I. Fitzgerald, Timothy 1950–   II. Lysik, David A.   III. Notre
Dame Center for Pastoral Liturgy. Conference (27th:1999)

   BX2215.A1 I53 2000
   264'.02—dc21   00-025090
                                              CIP

ISBN 1-56854-355-7
NCONG

Contents

Authors

Timothy Fitzgerald, a priest of the diocese of Des Moines, Iowa, is past associate director of the Notre Dame Center for Pastoral Liturgy. He is the current director of the Office of Adult Faith Formation and Lay Ministry for the diocese of Des Moines, and writes regularly on liturgy and prayer.

Melissa Musick Nussbaum is a teacher, lecturer, and the author of four books and numerous articles on liturgy and faith formation. She is the campus minister for the Catholic community at Colorado College in Colorado Springs. She and her husband are the parents of five children.

Peter C. Phan, PhD, STD, DD, is the Warren-Blanding professor of religion and culture in the department of religion and religious education at the Catholic University of America.

Richard S. Vosko, PhD, is a priest of the diocese of Albany, and has worked as a consultant and a designer of worship environments for 30 years. His projects continue to receive awards for liturgical and design excellence.

Introduction

There is in the Christian experience a nagging stretch between the present and the future, between the ideal and the real, between who we are and who we are called to be. The language of our liturgy echoes this tension—"Until Jesus, our Savior, comes again, we proclaim the work of your love" (Eucharistic Prayer for Masses for Various Needs and Occasions). Thus it has ever been. We live in the present, while our hearts and spirits dream of something beyond.

We take different measure of the resulting distance: The realist discounts the dreams, the idealist utterly depends upon them; the optimist believes that we inevitably advance toward the Promised Land, the pessimist knows that we are assured of a broken heart along the way.

Both the optimist and the pessimist are right about the journey of faith: the vision of life according to God's ways always compels us, but we will not reach the vision without suffering. Still, ought we to be paralyzed if the vision and the reality do not match? They seldom do. It is the visions—of a kingdom of peace, of a renewed church, of a compelling liturgy, of "full, conscious and active participation"—that fire the imagination and rekindle hope for each generation. We hold to our visions and our dreams, for they help us to remember and so to take heart and so to trust again. Our visions create hope, and hope always creates possibilities.

In August 1959, the twentieth North American Liturgical Week was held at the University of Notre Dame. The conference, "Participation in the Mass," drew nearly 3,500 participants. The names of its presenters and organizers form a litany of heralds and visionaries—McManus, Diekmann, Hellriegel, Theophane, Perkins Ryan, Burbach, Miriam Therese, Luykx, Hillenbrand, Ellard, Reed Newland, Marx, Sloyan, Walsh. We are surely heirs of those early promoters and pastoral ministers who were so eager to renew the liturgy and therefore renew the church. Many of their motivations we share in our own generation: The desire for "full, conscious and active participation" of all the baptized in the liturgy of the church and in the entire life of the church.

The liturgical week was framed by the deaths of figures important to liturgical life and renewal—Pius XII ten months before, and Fr. Michael Mathis, who initiated liturgical studies at Notre Dame in 1948, six months after. But the liturgical gathering also overlapped with incredible signs of life. On January 25 of that year, the recently elected John XXIII first proposed convening a church council. After a Mass for Christian unity at the basilica of St. Paul,

> the pope gathered around him the eighteen cardinals present for the occasion, [and] told them he had decided to call a council. Then he turned to the cardinals and said simply: "I would like your advice." The cardinals to a man sat mute before him. Not a single word of response was uttered.
>
> The pope has candidly recorded his disappointment: "Humanly we could have expected that the cardinals might have crowded around to express approval and good wishes." Yet he put the kindest and most charitable light on their unanimous failure to show any immediate reaction: "Instead there was a devout and impressive silence. Explanations came on following days." (Xavier Rynne, *Letters from Vatican City. Vatican Council II (First Session): Background and Debates*. New York: Farrar, Straus and Company, 1963; 2.)

Behold the incongruous Christian experience—signs of life and signs of death coincide and collide. When the Liturgical Week participants gathered in August 1959, they could not have foreseen what the next few years would contain. The bishop of Fort Wayne, Indiana, welcomed the participants "to a convention which is so much more than a convention, in the conventional sense of the word, which is held for such a high and holy purpose." (The Liturgical Conference, *Participation in the Mass*. Washington, D.C., 1960, 1). The Council convened October 11,1962, and we have lived with its vision ever since.

Most Catholics embraced the vision of a renewed and renewing church with enthusiasm; some never quite trusted it. The bishop who had welcomed the Liturgical Week cast a skeptical eye upon the Council and its impact. At their state convention in the early 1970s, he reminded the Knights of Columbus (and the rest of his diocese) that "we may be a 'pilgrim people,' but a pilgrimage is not a picnic!"

Still, the vision persists. In June 1999, 40 years after "Participation in the Mass," people gathered on the same campus for another pastoral liturgy conference. The Notre Dame Center for Pastoral Liturgy hosted its twenty-seventh conference, "Preparing the Church for the Liturgy."

The conference organizers called upon three people to ponder this vexing space we the church inhabit—the space between the visions and the reality. The fruits of their efforts are provided in this volume. Their perspectives on our liturgy and our life as church, fashioned by distinct life experiences and life works, are unique and complementary.

Peter Phan, president of the Catholic Theological Society of America, is an "academic" theologian who teaches at The Catholic University, Washington, D.C. His wise words consider how the church is to be formed *in order to come to* the eucharistic table *and* how the church is to form the world *because of* the eucharistic table. What is and what ought to be the relationship of how we worship and how we live?

Melissa Musick Nussbaum is, by acclamation, a "domestic" theologian. She firmly believes that if grace cannot be found and shared at the kitchen table, it cannot be found and shared at the eucharistic table. Why, then, she asks, do we rush to include family members at the kitchen table but dither about bringing them to the eucharistic table? Why can't the kitchen table and the eucharistic table shed light upon each other? Why are our gatherings at these tables—both tables of thanksgiving—so incongruous?

Richard Vosko surely qualifies as a "spatial" theologian whose insights are spun out in three-dimensional fashion. He has shared his passion for the worship of the church with worshiping communities throughout North America, helping them to craft space worthy of the church at prayer. Teacher, consultant, designer and writer, Richard Vosko urges the church to enflesh in its worship space the bold vision that has guided us for more than a generation—the full, conscious and active participation of the whole assembly in the worship of the church. Isn't God's house our house, too?

Each in turn, from different perspectives and experiences yet from a common love for the liturgy and the church, explores the space between the visions and the realities, the space in which we the church "live and move and have our being," a space marked with contradictions and incongruities. These three people, like the rest of us, often can do no more than to name the discrepancies. They cannot resolve them all.

But they also draw us back, with fresh insights and startling images, to the visions that create hope and the hope that creates possibilities. The wisdom of our tradition is that we experience the reality of church most clearly and fully in the church gathered and gathering for eucharist. Church and eucharist reflect each other, form and inform each other, shape each other. What we do at eucharist affects what we become as church, and how we live as church anticipates and reiterates how we are as the eucharistic assembly. That is our faith, the faith of the church.

This collection celebrates the liturgy that gives us life, and the life that shapes our liturgy. Walk with these wise people as guides, "in order to prepare ourselves to celebrate the sacred mysteries."

The Liturgy of Life as the "Summit and Source" of the Eucharistic Liturgy: Church Worship as Symbolization of the Liturgy of Life?

The question mark after the subtitle of this essay is not a cheap rhetorical flourish to attract the reader's attention. Rather, it is intended to highlight the tentative if not controversial character of the thesis proposed in this essay, namely, that the "liturgy of life" is the "summit and source" of the Christian liturgy. The phrase "summit and source" *(culmen et fons)* is of course taken from Vatican II's Constitution on the Liturgy *Sacrosanctum Concilium* (SC). The word "liturgy" is used here not univocally but analogously. What "liturgy" and "eucharist" are has been explained by the Council; what is meant by the "liturgy of life" and "symbolization" will be developed in this essay.

The thesis that the liturgy of life is the summit and source of the eucharistic liturgy, and not the other way around, is presented not as a straightforward assertion but as a genuine *quaestio disputata* regarding the relationship between worship and life. Needless to say, this issue is no irrelevant speculation for ivory-tower theologians; rather it entails far-reaching implications for the pastoral task of preparing the church for worship. In what follows, I will first discuss Vatican II's teaching that the liturgy is *culmen et fons* of the church's activities. Second, I will explore the basis for the alternative thesis that the liturgy of life is the summit and source of the eucharistic liturgy. Finally, I will examine the nature and function of one of the celebrations of the liturgy of life, namely, popular religion.

The Church's Liturgy as Summit and Source

The Teaching of Vatican II

That the liturgy is *culmen et fons* has become something of a mantra among post-Vatican II liturgists. The full text of article 10 of the *Constitution on the Liturgy,* in which the terms occur, reads:

> Nevertheless, the liturgy is the summit [culmen] toward which the activity of the church is directed; it is also the source [fons] from which all its power flows. For the goal of apostolic endeavor is that all who are made children of God by faith and Baptism should come together to praise God in the midst of God's church, to take part in the sacrifice and to eat the Lord's Supper.
>
> The liturgy, in its turn, moves the faithful filled with "the paschal sacraments" to be "one in their commitment to you"; it prays that "they hold fast in their lives to what they have grasped by their faith." The renewal in the Eucharist of the covenant between them and the Lord draws the faithful and sets them aflame with Christ's compelling love. From the liturgy, therefore, and especially from the Eucharist, grace is poured forth upon us as from a fountain [ut e fonte], and our sanctification in Christ and the glorification of God to which all other activities of the church are directed, as toward their end [utiad finem], are achieved with maximum effectiveness [maxima cum efficacia].[1]

Article 10 of SC should be read in the context of articles 9 through 13 which, *taken as a whole,* explain the relation of the liturgy to the whole of church life. On the one hand—against those who so exaggerate the importance of the liturgy as to identify it with the whole church life—article 9 affirms that "[t]he sacred liturgy is not the church's only activity." Examples are given of other kinds of necessary church activities: missionary preaching to unbelievers; spiritual preparation of believers for the sacraments by means of catechesis; works of charity, piety and the apostolate. On the other hand—against those who minimize the importance of the liturgy—article 10 asserts that it is both the "summit toward which the activity of the church is directed" and the "source from which all its power flows." However, for liturgical celebrations to achieve their full effects, article 11 urges that participants come to them "with proper dispositions" and that pastors aim not only at ensuring a valid and licit celebration but also at enabling the faithful to "take part fully aware of what they are doing, actively engaged in the rite and enriched by it." Once again, against liturgical enthusiasts, article 12 warns that "[t]he spiritual life, however, is not limited solely to participation in the liturgy" but includes also community prayers, private prayer and spiritual discipline. Article 13 even singles out popular devotions *(pia exercitia)* as "highly recommended."

Of the five articles of SC that elucidate the relationship between the liturgy and church life, only one affirms that the liturgy is summit and source, and even that affirmation is carefully qualified by the other four. This fact alone demands that we keep the statement about the liturgy as summit and source in proper perspective and balance. This refusal to absolutize the liturgy is confirmed by the history of the composition of article 10. During the Council, many Fathers expressed their misgivings about the affirmation that the liturgy is "the summit toward which the activity of the church is directed and the source from which all its power flows," and proposed amendments to it during the final vote on the chapter. In the text that the Central Commission submitted to the Council, the sentence was modified to say that "in its center, that is, in the divine sacrifice of the Eucharist" the liturgy is the summit and source. But even this milder formulation aroused objections during the assembly. It was pointed out that not even the eucharist can be said to be that to which everything is ordered and from which everything proceeds.

However, Auxiliary Bishop Jenny, who had been a member of the Preparatory Commission, insisted on retaining the original version with its comprehensive statement. The Council Commission approved his proposal and article 10 as it now stands in the Constitution was accepted by the Council by a vote of 2004 to 101.

But even those who endorsed the formula in the final vote explained in their proposed amendments why there was resistance to it. The summit and goal of the activity of the church, they argued, is not the liturgy but the salvation of souls and the glory of God. Furthermore, the highest virtue is not religion, which is realized in worship, but love. The liturgy is a means and not an end of church life. Finally, it was pointed out, the source of church life is not the liturgy but Christ and the Holy Spirit.[2] These various observations will serve as useful cautions against taking the affirmation about the liturgy as *culmen et fons* of the church's activities *sic et simpliciter.* Rather, the statement (as any other theological affirmation) must be taken *cum grano salis.*

What are the reasons for affirming that the liturgy is both the summit and the source of all the church's activities? Though not providing a comprehensive justification for its statement, SC does offer elements for an answer to this question. The first reason for the exalted dignity of the liturgy (as *culmen*/summit) lies no doubt in its very nature. Liturgy is an exercise of the priestly office of Jesus Christ *(veluti Iesu Christi sacerdotalis muneris exercitatio)*. It involves the presentation of humanity's sanctification under the guise of signs perceptible by the senses and its accomplishments in ways appropriate to each of these signs. In the liturgy, full public worship *(integer cultus publicus)* is performed by the Mystical Body of Jesus Christ, that is by the head and his members. From this it follows that every liturgical celebration, because it is an action of Christ the priest and of his body which is the church, is sacred action surpassing all others *(actio sacra praecellenter)*. No other action of the church can equal its efficacy by the same title and to the same degree *(eodem titulo eodemque gradu)*(SC, 7).

The liturgy's unsurpassed value is said to derive from the fact that it is a sacred action performed by the Mystical Body of Jesus Christ, which includes Christ as the head and the church as members.

Peter C. Phan

But in what sense is the liturgy the summit toward which the activities of the church are directed? Is it in the sense that the liturgy constitutes the end of the church's life? It seems not, since article 10 further specifies that all the activities of the church are directed not to the liturgy but to "our sanctification in Christ and the glorification of God . . . *as toward their end*" (emphasis added). It is only *indirectly* that the liturgy can be said to be the *culmen* to which the activities of the church are directed, insofar as it is the action by which the church accomplishes its twin task of glorifying God and being the sacrament of salvation to all humanity. Well-taken, therefore, is the point of the above-mentioned amendments of many Council Fathers who objected to the original formula on the ground that the liturgy is a means and not the end, and that the goal and summit of the church's activities is not the liturgy but the glory of God and the salvation of souls.

The second reason for the liturgy's unsurpassed excellence is its "efficacy." No other action of the church is said to equal its efficacy "by the same title and to the same degree." "By the same title" means that the efficacy of the liturgical celebrations is brought about by Christ himself who is their agent so that "when anyone baptizes, it is really Christ himself who baptizes" (SC, 7). "To the same degree" refers to the fact that in the liturgical celebrations the glorification of God and the salvation of souls "are achieved with maximum effectiveness" (SC, 10). In theological parlance, the efficacy of the liturgy is said to be by way of *ex opere operato* and not *ex opere operantis*. It is for this reason that SC says that the liturgy is "far superior" to any popular devotion (# 13).

With reference to the eucharist in particular, SC describes it as "a memorial of his [Jesus'] death and resurrection: a sacrament of love, a sign of unity, a bond of charity, 'a paschal banquet in which Christ is received, the mind is filled with grace, and a pledge of future glory is given to us'" (# 47). Because of what it is, the eucharist has been declared to be "the source and summit of the christian life *[totius vitae christianae fontem et culmen].*"[3] Elsewhere, the Council powerfully affirms the centrality of the eucharist for the life of the church and explains the reason for it:

[T]he other sacraments, and indeed all ecclesiastical ministries and works of the apostolate are bound up with the Eucharist and are directed towards it *[cum Eucharistia cohaerent et ad eam ordinantur]*. For in the most blessed Eucharist is contained the entire spiritual wealth of the church, namely Christ himself our Pasch and our living bread, who gives life to people through his flesh—that flesh which is given life and gives life by the Holy Spirit. Thus people are invited and led to offer themselves, their works and all creation in union with Christ. For this reason the Eucharist appears as the source and the summit of all preaching of the Gospel *[ut fons et culmen totius evangelizationis]*.[4]

The reason for the supreme excellence of the eucharist, then, lies in the special presence of Christ "in the eucharistic species" (SC, 7), although this "real presence" is to be understood together with Christ's presence in the person of his minister, the word of God, and the assembly of the worshiping faithful.

Theological Interpretations and Pastoral Applications

Vatican II's ringing affirmation of the liturgy and especially the eucharist as the summit and source of the church's life and activities has not remained empty rhetoric. On the contrary, it has deeply influenced the theological interpretation of the faith and shaped the pastoral practices of the church. On the level of theology, the eucharist has served as a lens through which almost all the doctrines of the faith are systematically re-examined and elaborated, from the Trinity through ecclesiology to eschatology. In pastoral practice, Sunday Masses are the focal points around which the life of the parish revolves. Pastors, associate pastors, permanent deacons, ushers, choir members, musicians, altar boys and altar girls, lectors, eucharistic ministers, members of the parish council, catechists, youth ministry directors, parish bulletin writers, collections receivers and counters, sacristans—nobody in the parish is left out of the all-consuming production of what we call the Sunday liturgy. The parish building complex, which is relatively deserted on weekdays, wakes up from its slumber on Sunday mornings to become the gathering circle of the parish community, with the pastor nervously timing the length of his homily so as not to create a traffic jam in the parking lot among those leaving one Mass and those driving in for another. Those who come from countries where attendance at Sunday Mass is often minimal and where liturgical celebrations are more often than not a dingy affair, will recognize that the Catholic church in the United States truly practices what the Council said about eucharistic celebrations as the summit and source of the life of the church.

While the centrality of eucharistic celebrations in American parishes is a source of legitimate pride for American Catholics, it is possible to ask whether the doctrine, which states that the liturgy is the summit and source of the church life, though theologically justified, has not led to one-sided theological interpretations and skewed pastoral practices. I would like to mention three areas where distortions may occur. They have to do with the two metaphors *culmen* and *fons* themselves.

First, the image of "summit" suggests a mountain or a pyramid and is symptomatic of the kind of epistemology that Ian Barbour identifies as the medieval paradigm that emphasizes fixed order, teleology, substance, hierarchy, anthropocentrism, dualism and kingdom in contrast to the post-modern paradigm that stresses evolution and historical emergence, structure and openness, mutual relation and interdependence, systems and wholes, organicism, multi-leveled composition and community.[5] Viewing the liturgy, and in particular the eucharist, as the summit toward which all the life of the church is ordered sets up a scale of values and willy-nilly devalues all other activities, ecclesial or otherwise, that do not qualify as liturgical and sacramental. This has happened, as we shall see, with popular devotions, which are placed at the bottom of the ladder of spiritual activities because their efficacy is said to be not ex *opere operato,* and not even *ex opere operantis ecclesiae.*

Within sacramental theology itself, even if it is granted that the eucharist is the *culmen* and *fons* of the church life, it has been debated whether it is more fundamental than, for example, baptism. Interestingly enough, it is not by accident that those who favor baptism over the eucharist often regard the universal priesthood conferred by baptism on all Christians as the basis for the possibility of the ordination of women to the ministerial priesthood. Whereas when the eucharist is granted primacy, the celebration of which implies hierarchical distinction with the priest alone acting *in persona Christi,* an argument is made to justify the exclusive reservation of the ministerial priesthood to males. The question here is not to deny the centrality of the eucharist for church life, but to search for a metaphor that fosters fundamental equality, mutual relationship, reciprocal dependence, openness, change and novelty in the way the liturgy and the eucharist interact with the other activities of the church.

Second, the metaphor of *fons* underlines the one-way relation between the original source and the body of water that flows out of it. However small is the source and however large is the river flowing down from it, there is only one way in which the two are related to one another, and that is, from the top to the bottom, and never from the bottom to the top. The water of the mighty river and its tributaries never flows backward, much less upward, to its source at the top of the mountain for which the image of *culmen* stands. Thus, the metaphor of "source" or "fountain" systematically excludes any possibility of fecundation and enrichment of the liturgy and the eucharist by other forms of worship or sacramental celebration, let alone popular devotions and daily life in general. Unlike the artificial fountains that grace our cities and buildings, whose water gushes upward reflecting the colors of the spectrum only to fall back down to the basin to be driven upward again to feed a continuous and perpetual watery arch, the image of the liturgy and the eucharist as *fons* conjures up no visions of returning movement, helpful feedback, mutual confrontation and reciprocal enrichment between worship and life. The movement is exclusively downstream, or as SC puts it, "[f]rom the liturgy, therefore, and especially from the Eucharist, grace is poured forth upon us as from a fountain" (# 10). Once again, the question is not to deny the fact that the liturgy and the eucharist are the conduits of divine life for us, but to devise a metaphor that intimates a continuous dynamic of mutual correction and fertilization between worship and life.

Third, underlying these two metaphors and their conceptions of liturgy and the eucharist is a particular theology of the relationship of God to the world (theology of grace) and of human beings (anthropology) that dominated the Catholic theological scene during the post-Tridentine era and residues which still linger in Vatican II's documents. With unavoidable over-generalizations, it may be said that this theology views Christians as living in two different and separate worlds, the "secular" and the "sacred." The larger world, the world of everyday life, the world of Monday through Saturday and even the greater part of Sunday, is secular and devoid of grace because it is only "nature" and worse, fallen and sinful. Only occasionally and at discreet points in time and space, by means of the sacraments and through worship, is it possible for Christians to encounter God and grace. This encounter, however, requires the Christians to leave the secular world behind, at least for a while, and enter the sacred temple to experience God's grace, and then fortified by God's gracious intervention, return to the fallen and unredeemed world. In this view, nature and grace are seen as forming the two separate levels of a two-story house, with grace on top of nature and even building on it, but never quite belonging to it and penetrating it.

In this view it is possible to establish a hierarchy whereby things of the world can be graded according to the degree of their proximity to the sacred temple. This scale of value is implied in the statement that the liturgy, especially the eucharist, is the summit and source of the church life. The eucharist is pictured as the fountain from which streams of grace cascade over the different regions of the spiritually parched world, more or less distant from it. Though watered by grace, the secular world is never brought into the sacred temple, nor is the temple built in the midst of the world. The assumption is that grace is an absolutely free gift of God only if it is parsimoniously and sporadically given to the sinful world, which otherwise is normally deprived of it.

These three distortions are no innocuous musings; on the contrary, they have deleterious effects on spiritual and pastoral practices. Three areas may serve as examples. In all three, there is a gaping dichotomy. The first is the dichotomy between liturgy and spirituality, the second between spirituality and socio-political involvement, and the third, to close the circle, between socio-political involvement and liturgy.[6]

In spite of the efforts of Vatican II to integrate spirituality and liturgy, in the post-conciliar years the old dualism, and of late the old clericalism, have crept back, sometimes with a vengeance. The reason for this unexpected turn of events is the metaphors of *culmen* and *fons* and their implicit theology separating church and world, worship and life, liturgy and spirituality, clergy and laity. In the immediate post-Vatican II era, liturgical experts were busy relocating altars, composing new liturgical texts, introducing vernacular languages, devising new rituals, et cetera—all very useful things indeed, only on the condition that they are rooted in the "liturgy of life," which alone, as I will show in the next part of the essay, provides them with meaning and effectiveness. Uprooted from the liturgy of life, these reforms appear as no more than clever gimmicks, concocted by the Vatican and imposed on the rest of Christendom, to cover up the vast irrelevance of the liturgical celebrations for everyday, real life. The famous phrase *ubi Christus, ibi ecclesia,* where Christ is, there is the church, or to apply it to our context, where the liturgy of life is, there is church worship, is reversed to read *ubi ecclesia, ibi Christus,* where the church is, there is Christ, or to apply it again to our context, where church worship is, there is the liturgy of life (which is of course not necessarily true).

The second dichotomy between spirituality and socio-political involvement shatters the synthesis that Ignatius of Loyola elaborated between contemplation and action. Rather than permanently yoked to action and nourished by it, contemplation is elevated to being a God-experience reserved to the few elite mystics, mostly clerics and religious, and confined to the sacred temple or the monastery, and is set in opposition to action, which is equated exclusively with concern for the world. The result is that contemplation is turned into a leisurely, harmless exercise in an ashram or retreat center to which those who can afford the luxury withdraw to commune with nature and soothe their bruised egos. Action is cut off from the source of its effectiveness, and Christians become nothing more than social workers.

The third dichotomy completes the circle. It isolates the liturgy from socio-political commitment and vice versa. The liturgy then becomes mere aesthetic performances, redolent with incense and dazzling with colorful vestments, perhaps accompanied by a full orchestra, a polyphonic choir and even Gregorian chant. The body and blood of Christ are then reduced to being the spiritual nourishment for the soul, and cease to be the bread and the drink feeding and slaking

Peter C. Phan

the poor and the hungry. On the other hand, separated from the church liturgy, socio-political involvement loses its religious dimension and ceases to be the "secular liturgy" that it is.

With these dichotomies playing havoc with church life and church worship, no wonder those responsible for preparing the parish for the liturgy spare no time, money and labor to make it a meaningful and relevant event. No wonder also that on Sundays, after the "shows" are over, all those involved in preparing the liturgy—from the presider, to the liturgy coordinator, to the choir director, to the minister of communion—breathe a collective sigh of relief, if not collapse in utter exhaustion, only to begin again on Monday mornings the rounds of preparation for the next Sunday liturgy.

And yet, despite the gargantuan efforts, the long-term effects of Sunday worship on the lives of the faithful seem like a momentary "high" at best and a blip on the screen at worst. The reason for this is, as we have seen, the chasm separating the church liturgy from the liturgy of life. Perhaps it is precisely this separation, and not any profound theological underpinning, that makes the eucharist appear as the summit and source of the church life for most people. Ironically, continuing to talk about eucharistic celebrations as the summit and source perpetuates and widens this chasm. Contemporary secular culture offers interesting parallels to this irony. Because the parents' lives are so much disconnected from those of their children, there is emphasis on parents spending "quality time" with their offspring, whereas such a need scarcely arises when their lives are deeply intertwined with each other. Because the human body has lost its sexual appeal due to overexposure, Victoria's Secret can make millions of dollars off their minimalist sartorial creations, advertising them to our saturated imagination as "sexy outfits," which would scarcely be necessary for those for whom the body is charged with innate erotic power. Because our daily meals are no longer occasions for sharing and friendship and communion, pricey restaurants can lure us with their promises of "a candlelit, romantic dinner for two," which would hardly be a necessity for real lovers. Quality time, sexy outfits and romantic dinners are the secular equivalents of the eucharist as "summit and source" that our consumerist culture attempts to purvey as substitutes for genuine care, authentic appreciation of the erotic and committed love. Only in a culture that has lost the sense of the liturgy of life can these *ersatz* products be passed off as genuine articles.

Church Worship as Symbolization of the Liturgy of Life

Something akin to a Copernican revolution in theology and pastoral practice is needed in order to revitalize church worship. While this may be an exaggeration, there is no doubt that a paradigm shift is involved. What is being advanced here is the reverse of Vatican II's adage. It is the *liturgy of life* that is the summit and source of the church liturgy and not the other way around.

The Whole World as Graced by the Self-Communication of God

One of Karl Rahner's fundamental theological principles is that God's grace, in the form of God's self-communication, has embraced and pervaded the world since its very beginning.[7] This gift is not *from* but *of* God, and is present in our history in two modes. The first is by way of an *offer* of God's self-gift, which has truly transformed our nature by making us capable of being united with God in grace. The second mode is by way of an *acceptance* or a *rejection* by us. If accepted, it will bring us into specifically distinct relationships with each of the three divine persons. If rejected, it will not be withdrawn but still remains as an offer. In either mode, whether as an offer or as an acceptance (or rejection) God's self-gift (grace) is present always and everywhere in our history.

According to Rahner, we are essentially oriented to God, who is the ever-recessive horizon of all our acts of knowing and loving. In every act of knowledge and love, we necessarily transcend ourselves and the concrete objects that we know and love and reach out toward, and anticipate the infinite horizon against which these objects are known and loved and which is therefore the pre-condition of our knowledge and love, but which forever eludes our grasp.[8] This self-transcendence in knowledge and love makes us capable of hearing a word of revelation from God if God chooses to speak to us (our *potentia obedientialis*).[9] However, because of God's actual self-communication to us in history, God, who is the absolute, ever-elusive, and distant Mystery, has come near us, irrevocably and supremely in Jesus Christ, becoming for us not only the Absolute but also the Holy Mystery, the God not only of infinite distance but also absolute closeness and immediacy. As a result of this divine self-gift, there is in us, as an intrinsic and constitutive part of our being, what Rahner calls the "supernatural existential," that is, a real, ontological modification of our nature that orients us toward union with God and the beatific vision. It is called an "existential" (the term borrowed from Martin Heidegger) because it is something not extrinsic but intrinsic to and constitutive of our nature; and it is "supernatural" because it is a gratuitous gift of God that cannot be demanded by our nature and therefore is not part of our essence. It is an *a priori* condition, pre-existing every act of choice of ours, which disposes us for a personal union with the triune God. As Rahner writes:

> The world is permeated by the grace of God . . . . The world is constantly and ceaselessly possessed by grace from its innermost roots, from the innermost personal center of the spiritual subject. It is constantly and ceaselessly sustained and moved by God's self-bestowal even prior to the question (admittedly always crucial) of how creaturely freedom reacts to this "engracing" of the world and of the spiritual creature as already given and "offered," the question, in other words, of whether this creaturely freedom accepts the grace to its salvation or closes itself to it to its perdition.[10]

In Rahner's view, then, human history and the world are totally and completely permeated by God's grace. Strictly speaking, therefore, there are no secular and sacred zones in human history, no profane marketplace and holy temple, but only the saved (where God's self-gift is accepted) and the damned (where it is rejected). This does not mean that Rahner compromises the gratuitousness of God's grace. He still maintains the logical necessity of the concept of "pure nature" to preserve the gratuitousness of grace, though "pure nature" has never existed in fact. Grace does not cease to be grace even when it is poured out upon everybody, always and everywhere, lavishly and abundantly.

Experience of God and Mysticism in Everyday Life

One important corollary of this theology of grace is that experiences of God and even mystical experiences are not seen as rare, much less confined to liturgical celebrations. On the contrary, since in every act of knowing and loving a particular object, we necessarily transcend ourselves and reach out toward the absolute horizon of being and value, and since this self-transcendence is permeated by the supernatural existential, experiences of God and grace are inescapable. These experiences of God do *not* occur *in addition to* or *apart from* our acts of knowing and loving particular objects, rather they lie hidden within them as their very condition of possibility. To distinguish these two levels of experiences, Rahner calls our knowledge and love of particular things "categorical," "thematic," "explicit" and "objective," and the experience of God "transcendental," "unthematic," "implicit" and "unobjective." Because of the hidden character of experiences of God, we are normally not aware of them, but our chronic inability to see God in everyday life is no indication that God is absent from it but rather that God is *radically* present in it in the literal sense of the word, that is, at the root, so that we who are habituated to perceiving life only at its surface, cannot see God at its depth.

By the same token, for Rahner, mystical experiences are not the preserve of the spiritual elite but are available to everyone. Of course they can occur in extraordinary phenomena such as visions, glossolalia, prophecies, ecstasies, dreams and the like, and these are not given to everyone. But mysticism has fundamentally to do with our self-transcendence and is basically an experience of the absolute mystery of God. So, says Rahner, "if we want to describe as 'mysticism' this experience of transcendence in which humans in the midst of ordinary life [are] always beyond themselves and beyond the particular object with which they are concerned, we might say that mysticism always occurs, concealed and namelessly, in the midst of ordinary life and is the condition of the possibility for the most down-to-earth and most secular experience of ordinary life."[11]

What are the kinds of experiences in which mysticism, that is, the graced encounter with God, occurs? The following long passage from Rahner deserves full quotation for its marvelous richness and lyrical beauty:

> But one point must be emphasized about this grace to the extent that it proceeds from the innermost heart and center of the world and of the human person: it takes place not as a special phenomenon, as one particular process *apart from* the rest of human life. Rather it is quite simply the ultimate depths and the radical dimension of all that which the spiritual creature experiences, achieves and suffers in all those areas in which it achieves its own fullness, and so in its laughter and tears, in its taking responsibility, in its loving, living, and dying, whenever the person keeps faith with the truth, breaks through egoism in one's relationships with one's fellows, whenever one hopes against all hope, whenever one smiles and refuses to be disquieted or embittered by the folly of everyday pursuits, whenever one is able to be silent, and whenever within this silence of the heart that evil which a person has engendered against another in his or her heart does not develop any further into external action, but rather dies within this heart as its grave—whenever, in a word, life is lived as we would seek to live it, in such a way as to overcome our own egoism and the despair of the heart which constantly assails us. *There* grace has the force of an event, because all this is of its very nature (i.e. precisely through God's grace which has all along broken mere "nature," leading it beyond itself and into the infinitude of God) no longer has any limits or any end but (as willingly accepted) loses itself in the silent infinitude of God, is hidden in his absolute unconditionality in the future of the fullness of victory which in turn is God himself.[12]

It is clear that for Rahner experiences of God and mysticism are given to us in both a positive and negative light, perhaps more in the latter than in former, because then we are confronted with our own limitations and brought face to face with the infinite mystery. This means that there is nothing in life so profane and secular, so negative and evil, that God cannot be experienced in it.

Liturgy of Life

These universal experiences of God and mystical encounters with God's grace in the midst of everyday life, made possible by God's self-gift embracing the whole human history, always and everywhere, from what Rahner calls the "liturgy of the world" *(Liturgie der Welt)* or the "Mass of the world" *(Messe der Welt)*.[13] To underline its dynamic and personal character, one may prefer to call it the "liturgy of life." Rahner describes this liturgy of the world or of life as follows:

> The world and its history are the terrible and sublime liturgy, breathing of death and sacrifice, which God celebrates and causes to be celebrated in and through human history in its freedom, a history which God sustains in grace by his sovereign disposition. In the entire length and breadth of this immense history of birth and death, complete superficiality, folly, inadequacy, and hatred . . . on the one hand, and silent submission, responsibility even to death in dying and in joyfulness, in attaining the heights and plumbing the depths on the other, the true liturgy of the world is present. To this liturgy of the world the liturgy which the Son has brought to its absolute fullness on his cross belongs intrinsically, emerges from it, that is, from the ultimate source of the grace of the world, and constitutes the supreme point of *this* liturgy. All else draws its life from this supreme point, because everything else is always dependent upon the supreme point as upon its goal and is supported by it. This liturgy of the world is as it were veiled to the darkened eyes and the dulled human heart which fails to understand its true nature. This liturgy, therefore, must, if the individual is really to share in the celebration of it in all freedom and self-commitment even to death, be interpreted, "reflected upon" in its ultimate depths when one celebrates that which we are accustomed to call liturgy in the more usual sense. But there is a further point, just as valid and indeed still more radical: We can understand this liturgy in the usual sense and can achieve a genuine enactment of it . . . only if we draw our strength from this liturgy of the world, from the existential liturgy of faith which is identical with the history of the world rightly enacted.[14]

Peter C. Phan

From this description, four characteristics of the liturgy of life emerge. First, the liturgy of life consists of experiences of God, available to all human beings, in the midst of life and in all concrete situations, from the most sublime to the most mundane, both positive and negative. It is called "liturgy" because these experiences are always sustained by God's self-gift to the world. It is called "of the world" because it takes place in the universal history of the world which, according to Rahner, is "coextensive"(though not identical) with the history of salvation.[15] This "general" history of salvation is to be distinguished from the "special" history of revelation and salvation (i.e., the history of the Old and New Testaments), just as the liturgy of life is different from church liturgy and worship. Though less easily identifiable than the special history of salvation and church worship, the general history of salvation and its liturgy of life are no less real and important.

Second, this liturgy of the world has a christological character for two reasons. The first is that Jesus' sacrifice on the cross—or his liturgy—derived its origin or emerged from the liturgy of the world. For Rahner, the incarnation of the Word in Jesus, though a unique event, is "an intrinsic moment within the whole process by which grace is bestowed upon all spiritual creatures."[16] In other words, the incarnation of the Logos forms an intrinsic part of the process of God's self-communication to the world, the dynamic power of which prepared for it and without which it could not have happened: "Grace in all of us and hypostatic union in the one Jesus Christ can only be understood together, and as a unity they signify the one free decision of God for a supernatural order of salvation, for God's self-communication."[17] This thesis not only provides unity to the doctrines of creation and redemption but also coheres with an evolutionary view of the world in which matter is conceived of as actively transcending itself toward and becoming spirit. If humanity as the unity of matter and spirit can be considered as the goal of the cosmic evolution, then the incarnation of the Logos can rightly be said to be the highest actualization of the essence of human reality.[18] The second reason for the christological character of the liturgy of life is the fact that the incarnation, death and resurrection of the Logos brought it to its fullest fulfillment and constitute its supreme point.

Through these events God's self-communication in history became definitive, irrevocable, irreversible, insofar as it is now both *offer* and *acceptance* indissolubly united as one in the person of Jesus (that is what "hypostatic union" means). In this sense, Rahner suggests that Christ can be called the "Absolute Savior."[19]

Third, the liturgy of life is necessarily diffuse, unstructured, and therefore easily unnoticed. This characteristic flows from the transcendental nature of our experiences of God. The presence of God—silently present and silencing his presence—occurs as a nameless mystery in the depths of our everyday experiences and hence is frequently ignored, misinterpreted and even suppressed. Even when this divine presence is attended to, it can never be fully captured and communicated in conceptual categories. What is needed, according to Rahner, is mystagogy, that spiritual discipline whereby we are guided and formed to perceive beyond the surface of life the abiding presence of the absolute and holy Mystery.[20] One place where this mystagogy should be carried out in particular is church liturgical celebrations.

Fourth, though less visible than church liturgy, this liturgy of life is the very source of fecundity and effectiveness of the liturgy of the church. Indeed, humanity's ongoing communion with God in grace in daily life is, according to Rahner, the primary and original liturgy. It is this liturgy of life that we must first think of when we speak of worship. Worship is not primarily the explicit act of praise and thanksgiving we perform within the walls of the church away from the secular arena but the daily, silent, unobtrusive surrendering of ourselves to the infinite Mystery in our everyday action: ". . . the church's worship is not the installation of a primarily sacramental sphere in a profane, secular world, it is not an event otherwise without roots in reality, but the explicit and reflex, symbolic presentation of the salvation event which is occurring always and everywhere in the world; the liturgy of the church is the symbolic presentation of the liturgy of the world."[21]

Church Liturgy as "Real Symbol" of the Liturgy of Life

With the last quotation we have already broached the issue of how to articulate the relationship between the liturgy of life and church liturgy and in particular eucharistic celebrations. We have seen above the validity as well as the theological and pastoral limitations in the use of the metaphors of *culmen* and *fons* to express this relationship. One alternative way of conceiving it that retains the important role of liturgy and sacramental celebrations for the church life and yet eschews the distortions to which the metaphors of summit and source are liable is by way of Rahner's theology of the symbol.[22]

According to Rahner, a "real symbol," in contrast to an artificial sign, is a reality in which and by means of which another reality comes to be present and effective. Rahner applies this concept of real symbol to the doctrine of the Trinity, in which the Logos is said to be the symbol of the Father; to ecclesiology, in which the church is said to be the symbol of Christ; to sacramentology, in which the sacraments are said to be the symbols of the church; and to anthropology, where the body is said to be the symbol of the soul.[23]

Rahner also uses his theology of the symbol to explicate the relationship between the liturgy of life and the liturgy of the church. To put it in a nutshell, the liturgy of the church is the "real symbol" of the liturgy of life. There are several theological and pastoral implications in this thesis. First, as the thing symbolized and its symbol constitute an ontological and indissoluble unity, so the liturgy of life and the liturgy of the church constitute the one worship that humanity renders to God and whose center and supreme fulfillment is Jesus Christ. Conversely, just as the symbol and the thing symbolized preserve their irreducible distinctiveness and difference, so the liturgy of life is not identical with the liturgy of the church and vice versa. The one is not and should not be absorbed into the other.

Second, just as the thing symbolized comes to be real, present and effective in the symbol, so the liturgy of life comes to be real, present and effective in the liturgy of the church. Because the liturgy of life is diffuse and hidden in everyday ordinary experiences in the midst of life and therefore runs the risk of being ignored, it needs to be brought to our consciousness by being symbolized in the concrete and explicit rituals and prayers of the church worship and sacraments. The sacrament then "constitutes a small sign, necessary, reasonable and indispensable, within the infinitude of the world as permeated by God. It is the sign that reminds us of this limitlessness of the presence of divine grace, and *in this sense* and in no other, precisely in *this particular* kind of anamnesis, is to be intended to be an event of grace."[24]

Third, just as the symbol does not exist by itself and on its own but derives its being from the thing symbolized, so the liturgy of the church does not exist by itself and is not effective except as symbolization of the liturgy of life. The original liturgy is not the church liturgy but the liturgy of life. In its liturgical celebrations the church does not perform a worship *in addition to* the liturgy of life or unconnected with it; rather it makes explicit and intensifies through words and rituals the liturgy of life which takes place unceasingly through God's self-gift and humanity's acceptance of this divine self-gift. The value of the church liturgy is precisely in not identifying itself with or replacing the liturgy of life as the original and exclusive liturgy but in being its symbol by making it concretely present here and now in the consciousness of the faithful. The church liturgy is important not because what happens there does not happen elsewhere and not because what happens supremely there happens only as a shadow elsewhere. Rather, it is because what happens in the church liturgy happens always and everywhere in the world, but here it is explicitly celebrated, announced and appropriated. Consequently, says Rahner, "to anyone who has (or might have had) absolutely no experience in his own life of this history of grace in the world, no experience of the cosmic liturgy, the church's liturgy could only seem like a strange ritualism, as strange as the sacrificial action of a Vedic priest who feeds the gods and thinks that by his action he is keeping the world on its track."[25]

Fourth, just as the thing symbolized and its symbol are not related to each other by a hierarchical, one-way, top-to-bottom, static order, as implied in the metaphors of summit and source, but by a dynamic, two-way, mutual interdependence, so the liturgy of life and the liturgy of the church interact with each other as two intrinsic dimensions of the one reality, correcting and enriching each other. Contrary to Vatican II, which speaks of the liturgy of the church as the summit and source of all the activities of the church, the theology of the church liturgy as symbol of the liturgy of life does not speak of the church liturgy as summit and source. On the contrary, just as the thing symbolized is in a certain sense more original than its symbol, so it is the liturgy of life that is the more original and more fundamental, and in this sense could be said to be the summit and source of the church liturgy. To be more precise, the true summit, center and source of both the liturgy of life and the liturgy of the church is Jesus Christ who in his incarnation, ministry, death and resurrection brought God's self-communication to the world to its irrevocable, irreversible and victorious fulfillment. Consequently, with the liturgy of the church as the symbol of the liturgy of life, there is no dichotomy but mutual inclusion between spirituality and liturgy, between liturgy and socio-political involvement and between socio-political involvement and spirituality.

Finally, just as between the thing symbolized and its symbol there is no relation of efficient causality through which the one brings the other into existence by its own power, so between the liturgy of life and the liturgy of the church there is no relation of efficient causality by which one brings the other into existence *ex nihilo,* as if the one were totally dependent on the other without the other being in some measure also dependent on it. Rather between them there is a relationship of mutual dependence and reciprocal origination by which the one comes into being, being real, being effective through the other, the thing symbolized by expressing itself in the symbol, and the symbol by being the concrete embodiment of the thing symbolized. Indeed, this kind of formal causality is proper to the sacraments as *signum efficax* of grace: The liturgy of the church is the sign of the original liturgy of life and insofar as it is the sign of the liturgy of life that is sustained by the ever-present grace of God, it "causes" grace, that is, makes the grace of the liturgy of life concretely effective here and now for the worshiping community.

Popular Religion: Parallel Symbolization of the Liturgy of Life

In the light of the theology of the liturgy of life as the original liturgy, it would be useful to revisit the complex and controverted issue of popular religion or popular religiosity (in Spanish, *religiosidad popular*). It is of course impossible to offer within the remaining space of this essay anything remotely approaching an adequate theological treatment of popular religion, especially its relationship to the church liturgy. In the following reflections it will be suggested that popular religion can be best understood if it is viewed as a real symbol of the liturgy of life, in much the same way as the church liturgy symbolizes the liturgy of life.

Whether under the rubric of "popular religion," or "folk religion," or "common religion,"[26] it is well known that non-liturgical, non-official, popular expressions of religiosity ("popular" not in the sense of "in fashion," but "of the people in general") received scant attention from Vatican II. Article 13 of SC treats it only under the aspect of "popular devotions" *(pia exercitia)* and declares:

> The Christian people's devotions, provided they conform to the laws and norms of the church, are to be highly recommended, especially when they are authorized by the Apostolic See.
>
> Devotions authorized by bishops in particular churches according to lawfully approved customs or books are also held in special esteem.
>
> But such devotions should be so drawn up that they harmonize with the liturgical seasons, accord with the sacred liturgy, are in some way derived from it, and lead the people to it, since in fact the liturgy by its very nature is far superior to any of them.[27]

In the immediate post-Vatican II era, as the liturgical reform went into full swing, popular religion suffered a serious decline. All its four forms, as classified by Domenico Sartore, were affected: first, devotions to Christ, the Blessed Virgin, and the saints in the forms of pilgrimages, patronal feasts, processions, popular devotions and novenas; second, the rites related to the liturgical year; third, traditional practices in conjunction with the celebrations of the sacraments and other Christian rites like funerals; and fourth, institutions and religious objects connected with various forms of popular religiosity.[28]

Recently, however, there has been a noticeable resurgence of popular religion not only among the churches of the Third World, in particular Latin America and Asia,[29] but also among Christians of the First World.[30] One of the contributing factors to this comeback is the widespread dissatisfaction with the classical form of Vatican II's

Peter C. Phan

reformed rites—characterized by Roman *sobrietas, brevitas, simplicitas* and linear rationality—that does not respond to the people's need for emotional and total involvement in liturgical celebrations.[31] This need is met by popular religion with its emphasis on spontaneity, festivity, joyfulness and community.[32]

Besides the inadequacy of the Roman rites, SC's approach to popular religion is heavily legalistic. Popular devotions are said to be "highly recommended" only on condition that "they conform to the laws and norms of the church" and especially "when they are authorized by the Apostolic See." They have a special dignity "if they are authorized by bishops in particular churches according to lawfully approved customs or books." More importantly, the four norms that SC formulates for drawing up devotions, namely that "they harmonize with the liturgical seasons, accord with the sacred liturgy, are some way derived from it, and lead the people to it" are all derived from the principle that the liturgy is the summit and source of all activities of the church.[33] This principle, as we have seen above, can and does lead to distortions in both theology and pastoral practice.

Rather than seeing popular religion in direct relationship to the church liturgy that functions as its exclusive norm, I suggest we view popular religion as the symbolization of the liturgy of life, a symbolization that is parallel to the church liturgy's symbolization of the liturgy of life. Therefore, popular religion needs to be assessed on its own terms and not in dependence on the church liturgy. The function and value of popular religion lies not in its ability to "harmonize with the liturgical seasons," "accord with the sacred liturgy," be "in some way derived from it" and "lead people to it." Nor should popular religion be ranked at the bottom of the list of spiritual activities on the basis of its alleged efficacy being merely *ex opere operantis,* as opposed to *ex opere operato* (as with the liturgy and sacraments) and *ex opere operantis ecclesiae* (as with the sacramentals),[34] or because of its alleged "private" character as opposed to the "public" character of church worship.[35]

As symbol of the liturgy of life, popular religion is related to it in very much the same way as the church liturgy is. In brief, the liturgy of life and popular religion form the one worship rendered to God, though each retains its distinctive identity. The liturgy of life becomes real, effective and concrete in and through popular religion, just as popular religion achieves its effectiveness by being the real symbol of the liturgy of life. Between them there is a mutual causal relationship characterized not by efficient causality but by formal or symbolic causality.

In this understanding of popular religion, the negative approaches that regard popular religion either as mere superstitious practices (the elitist interpretation) or as the false consciousness imposed upon the proletariat by the ruling class (the Marxist interpretation), are discounted. On the other hand, this understanding of popular religion does not fall into romanticism by regarding popular religion as the genuine religion that has been skewed by official religion, or that now resides in the majority of the people who lead a poor and simpler life (the romanticist interpretation). Nor does it see popular religion as residues of the previous, pre-Christian religion that now survives in a transformed and improved state in Christianity (the remnant interpretation). Nor does it look upon popular religion mainly as articulation of the social-psychological needs of individuals in their interaction with the economic, social and political patterns of the environment (the social-psychological approach).

Stated positively, this approach to popular religion is similar to the baseline approach, proposed by Robert Towler, which recognizes that every culture has its own religious symbolization that takes place in two parallel forms, popular religion and organized world religions (each with their own official liturgy and worship). Both popular religion and official liturgy are distinct symbolizations of the liturgy of life; the one should not be identified with the other, or replaced by the other, or reduced to the other. This approach is also sympathetic to the subaltern approach, inspired by the Italian Marxist Antonio Gramsci, which sees popular religion as having an identity of its own, independent from the official religion with its own public worship, and capable of forging the identity of the oppressed people over the ruling class.[36]

Needless to say, this view of popular religion entails important implications for the issue of liturgical inculturation.[37] While it is impossible to spell out the details of this process of inculturation here, one thing is clear: Vatican II's wholesale subordination of popular religion to liturgy is no longer viable. Rather there should be "a mutual and enriching exchange between the liturgy and popular devotion,"[38] in the composition of texts and the establishment of rituals, because both are equally valid symbolizations of the liturgy of life. The liturgy of life is the first seed sown by God's gracious love, a seed that grows up and blossoms in the vicissitudes of human history, a seed not unlike the one celebrated by the Irish-American poet, William D. Carroll, as he recalled the wild grass and the wildflowers that grow in acres and acres of rock called the "Burren" in County Clare, Ireland:

A Seed

A seed did fall upon the ground
Where desolation did abound
A crack within a rock it found
And waited.

For winds that came from off a hill
With flecks of dust the crack to fill
And rain from out the sky did spill
And sated.

The little seed's great appetite.
And nurtured through long Winter's night
It waited for the Spring's sunlight
As fated.

The Winter melded into Spring
Bringing new life to everything
And nature's elemental sting
Abated.

Out from the rock a plant did sprout
Midst degradation all about
And to the universe did shout
Elated.

"I am the vanguard of a breed."
And as nature had decreed,
Upon the ground did fall a seed
And mated.[39]

1. All English translations of the documents of Vatican II are taken from *Vatican II: The Basic Sixteen Documents,* ed. Austin Flannery, OP (Northport NY: Costello Publishing Company, 1996), with slight modifications.

2. For a summary presentation of the composition of article 10, see Josef Andreas Jungmann, "Constitution on the Sacred Liturgy," in *Commentary on the Documents of Vatican II,* ed. Herbert Vorgrimmler, vol. 1 (Northpart NY: Costello Publishing Company, 1996), 15–16.

3. Vatican II, dogmatic constitution *Lumen Gentium* (On the Church) (LG), 11.

4. Vatican II, decree *Presbyterorum Ordinis* (on the ministry and life of priests) 5.

5. See Ian Barbour, *Religion in an Age of Science* (New York: Harper and Row), 219.

6. For an analysis of these dichotomies, see Aloysius Pieris, *An Asian Theology of Liberation* (Maryknoll NY: Orbis Books, 1988), 3–14. Pieris argues that only a genuine liberation theology can break this triple dichotomy that keeps these three elements apart from each other. It does so, he suggests, by refocusing the church's attention on the liturgy of life, the theology of the cross, and the historical Jesus and his humanity.

7. For Rahner's most important writings on grace, see his "Concerning the Relationship Between Nature and Grace," *Theological Investigations* (TI) 1 (Baltimore: Helicon, 1961), 297–317; "Some Implications of the Scholastic Concept of Uncreated Grace," TI 1 (Baltimore: Helicon, 1961), 319–46: "Nature and Grace," TI 4 (New York: Crossroad, 1982), 165–88; and *Foundations of Christian Faith: An Introduction to the Idea of Christianity,* trans. William Dych (New York: Seabury, 1978), 116–33. For a helpful study of Rahner's theology of worship, see Michael Skelley, *The Liturgy of the World: Karl Rahner's Theology of Worship* (Collegeville MN: The Liturgical Press, 1991).

8. See Karl Rahner, *Spirit in the World,* trans. William Dych (New York: Herder and Herder, 1968).

9. See Karl Rahner, *Hearers of the Word,* trans. Joseph Donceel (Milwaukee: Marquette University Press, 1982).

10. Karl Rahner, "Considerations on the Active Role of the Person in the Sacramental Event," TI 14, 166.

11. Karl Rahner, "Experience of the Holy Spirit," TI (New York: Crossroad, 1983), 197.

12. Karl Rahner, "Considerations on the Active Role of the Person in the Sacramental Event," TI 14, 167–68. See also Rahner's other essays: "Reflections on the Experience of Grace," TI 3 (New York: Crossroad, 1982), 86–90; "The Experience of God Today," TI 11 (New York: Crossroad, 1982), 149–65; "Experience of the Spirit and Existential Commitment," TI 16 (New York: Crossroad, 1983), 24–34; "Religious Feeling Inside and Outside the Church," TI 17

(New York: Crossroad, 1981), 213–38; "Experience of Transcendence from the Stand Point of Catholic Dogmatics," TI 18 (New York: Crossroad, 1983), 173–88; "Experience of the Holy Spirit," TI 18 (New York: Crossroad, 1983), 189–210.

13. Karl Rahner, "Considerations on the Active Role," TI 14, 174.

14. Karl Rahner, "Considerations on the Active Role of the Person in the Sacramental Event," TI 14, 170. For the idea of the liturgy of life Rahner refers to the works of Pierre Teilhard de Chardin, especially his book *Hymn of the Universe* (New York: Harper & Row, 1965). The expression "Mass of the World" is derived from Teilhard.

15. For Rahner's discussion of the relationship between the general and special histories of revelation and salvation, see his *Foundations of Christian Faith,* 138–161, 170–175.

16. Karl Rahner, *Foundations of Christian Faith,* 201.

17. Karl Rahner, *Foundations of Christian Faith,* 201.

18. For Rahner's proposal of a christology with an evolutionary worldview, see his *Foundations of Christian Faith,* 178–203.

19. See Karl Rahner, *Foundations of Christian Faith,* 193–95.

20. On mystagogy in Rahner, see James Bacik, *Apologetics and the Eclipse of Mystery: Mystagogy According to Karl Rahner* (Notre Dame IN: University of Notre Dame Press, 1980).

21. Karl Rahner, "On Theology of Worship," TI 19, 146.

22. For Rahner's theology of symbol, see his "The Theology of the Symbol," TI 4 (Baltimore: Helicon, 1966), 221–52 and "The Concept of Mystery in Catholic Theology," TI 4 (Baltimore: Helicon, 1966), 36–73.

23. See Karl Rahner, "The Theology of the Symbol," TI 4, 235–49.

24. Karl Rahner, "Considerations on the Active Role of the Person in the Sacramental Event," TI 14, 169.

25. Karl Rahner, "On the Theology of Worship," TI 19, 147.

26. For a helpful discussion of these terminologies and of popular religion in general, see Robert Schreiter, *Constructing Local Theologies* (Maryknoll NY: Orbis Books, 1985), 122–43. Popular religion is often contrasted to official religion, elite religion and esoteric religion. Schreiter rightly notes the inadequacy of these approaches and calls for an adherence in the studies of popular religion to the following principles: "trying to listen to the culture on its own terms; adopting a holistic pattern of description; remaining attentive to the audience and the interest of the questioner in each event" (126).

27. This relative neglect of and suspicious attitude toward popular religion by Vatican II was one of the results of the triumph of the Liturgical Movement,

spearheaded by Dom Prosper Gueranger, at the Council. The Liturgical Movement saw popular religion as rooted in subjective and emotional piety, thus favoring the individualist tendencies of the Enlightenment, tendencies Vatican II wanted to combat. This belittling of "subjective" or "personal" piety, and the consequent rejection of "all other religious exercises not directly connected with the sacred Liturgy and performed outside public worship," was criticized by Pope Pius XII as "false, insidious, and quite pernicious" (*Meditor Dei,* 30). Papal condemnations notwithstanding, the Liturgical Movement's negative assessment of popular religion found its way into article 13 of SC. See Patrick L. Malloy, "The Re-Emergence of Popular Religion Among Non-Hispanic American Catholics," *Worship* 72 (1998): 2–4.

28. See Anscar Chupungco, *Liturgical Inculturation: Sacramentals, Religiosity, and Catechesis* (Collegeville MN: The Liturgical Press, 1992), 102, summarizing D. Sartore, "Le manifestazione della religiosita popolare," *Anamnesis* 7 (Genoa, 1989): 232–33.

29. For an evaluation of popular religion from a Latin American perspective, see Michael R. Candelaria, *Popular Religion and Liberation: The Dilemma of Liberation Theology* (Albany NY: SUNY Press, 1990), and Cristian Parker, *Popular Religion & Modernization in Latin America: A Different Logic,* trans. Robert Barr (Maryknoll NY: Orbis Books, 1996). For studies of Hispanic-American popular religion, see Orlando Espin, *The Faith of the People: Theological Reflections on Popular Catholicism* (Maryknoll NY: Orbis Books, 1997), and C. Gilbert Romero, *Hispanic Devotional Piety* (Maryknoll NY: Orbis Books, 1991).

30. See Patrick L. Malloy, "The Re-Emergence of Popular Religion Among Non-Hispanic American Catholics," *Worship* 72, 1 (1998): 5–8. Just to have an idea of how this re-emergence has spawned an avalanche of literature on popular religion, a bibliography composed in 1979 showed that in the previous decade there had been 528 titles. See F. Trolese, "Contributo per una bibliografia sulla religiosita popolare," *Ricerche sulla relgiosita popolare* (Bologna, 1979); 273–535. For other bibliographies, see Anscar Chupungco, *Liturgical Inculturation,* 95.

31. It is these characteristics that lie behind SC's insistence on a "full, conscious, and active participation in liturgical celebration" (# 14). For a critique of Vatican II's liturgical reform by four ideologically diverse theologians (Joseph Ratzinger, David Power, Francis Mannion and Matthew Fox) see Patrick L. Malloy, "The Re-Emergence of Popular Religion Among Non-Hispanic American Catholics," *Worship* 72 (1998): 12–20.

32. For a description of the general traits of popular religion, see Anscar Chupungco, *Liturgical Inculturation,* 109–111. Chupungco quotes C. Valenziano's characterization of popular religion: "It is festive, felt, spontaneous; it is expressive, immediate, human; it is communitarian, collective, joyful, symbolic, traditional, alive" (109–110). See C. Valenziano, "La religiosita popolare in prospettiva antropologica," in *Liturgia e religiosita popolare* (Bologna, 1979), 83–110. Chupungco, in his analysis of Filipino popular religion, identifies the principle features

of popular religion as follows: "These are, first, their literary genre, which is marked by discursive and picturesque quality; second, their use of sacred images; third, their preference for such devices for participation repetitiveness and communal recitation; and fourth, their use of dramatic forms that are often strongly mimetic or imitative" (119).

33. The same legalistic approach to popular religion is maintained in the instruction *Varietates legitimae* (Inculturation and the Roman Liturgy) issued by the Congregation for Divine Worship and the Discipline of the Sacraments (Rome, 1994). Article 45 says: "The introduction of devotional practices into liturgical celebrations under the pretext of inculturation cannot be allowed 'because by its nature, (the liturgy) is superior to them.' It belongs to the local Ordinary to organize such devotions, to encourage them as supports of the life and faith of Christians, and to purify them, when necessary because they need to be constantly permeated by the Gospel. He will take care to ensure that they do not replace liturgical celebrations or become mixed up with them."

34. Such a theological distinction is rendered quite fuzzy by the fact that even for the sacraments to produce their effects the "proper dispositions" of the recipient are necessary; after all, the sacraments are *sacramenta fidei*. Furthermore, in real life, sometime kissing a statue, going on a pilgrimage or making a novena can bring more spiritual transformation than celebrating the sacraments.

35. The distinction between "private" and "public" is also very fuzzy. Saying Mass in a hotel room or individual recitation of the breviary is no more "public worship" than a procession through the streets of the city. This distinction depends on the view that the church is more "sacred" than the public square.

36. For a helpful explanation of these seven approaches to popular religion, two negative (elitist and Marxist) and five positive (baseline, romanticist, remnant, subaltern, and social-political), see Robert Schreiter, *Constructing Local Theologies*, 131–39.

37. On the liturgical inculturation of popular religion, see Anscar Chupungco, *Liturgical Inculturation*, 95–133. Chupungco favors the method of dynamic equivalence (121–33). He distinguishes the method of dynamic equivalence (which he acknowledges is not "officially the exclusive method of inculturation [125]) from the method of introducing the various forms of popular religion into the liturgy (the method of inculturation) and from the method raising certain forms of popular religiosity to the status of a liturgical rite (the method of aggregation).

38. *Evangelization in Latin America's Present and Future*. Final Document of the Third General Conference of the Latin American Episcopate (Puebla de Los Angeles, Mexico, 1979), no. 465. See *Puebla and Beyond*, ed. John Eagleson and Philip Scharper (Maryknoll NY: Orbis Books, 1979), 188. Translation slightly revised.

39. William D. Carroll, *Songs Poems Perceptions* (Washington DC: Semone West Publishing Company, 1998), 72–73. Used with permission.

Melissa Musick Nussbaum

Have All Been Fed?

Are There Any in Need?

The baptized devoted themselves to the apostles' teaching and common life, to the breaking of bread and the prayers. . . . All who believed were together and had all things in common; they broke bread at home and ate their food with glad and generous hearts, praising God and having the goodwill of all the people.

This reading from the Acts of the Apostles (2:42, 44, 46b–47a), though we always hear it proclaimed at church, always makes me think of the home. Much like the life of the household, the reading is filled with verbs, with action: they *break* bread, they *eat* food, they *hold* all things in common, they *praise* God, they *pray*. Andrew Ciferni's phrase, "The preaching is the life" can be understood as: The life is the preaching. Parents know this well, perhaps because children come to them pre-verbal and pre-rational. It's no good telling an infant how much you love her if you aren't comforting her when she cries, changing her diapers when she is wet and feeding her when she is hungry. She won't understand your words. Yet she will soon apprehend that, when she is hungry, her mother's voice, her father's touch means that food is near, comfort is at hand, and she will begin to trust. The life is the preaching.

Of course, that means the life cruelly and carelessly lived is also the preaching. An infant may learn that his mother's voice is a scream for him to shut up; his father's touch a slap. Or, she may rarely hear her mother's voice; feel her father's touch. They are busy. And the child begins to mistrust, to fear and then to hate. The preaching is the life.

Melissa Musick Nussbaum

The life is the preaching. When I work with parents who are preparing their children for first communion, I always ask them first to talk about their households, to uncover the formation they are already doing, have been doing all along. And so, thinking of this common life, this breaking of bread at home, I ask, "When did you first bring this child to the family table?" Parents are surprised by the question because the answer seems so transparent and so obvious that they wonder why I would bother to ask it.

"The first time I returned to the table after giving birth," the mothers will say. And that will set us off, laughing and remembering the incredible three-person mealtime nursing juggling act: the hungry mother, always without a net, attempts to cradle the baby at her breast with one hand while she maneuvers a fork with the other, and her husband wields the dinner knife as necessary. How single mothers ever manage to eat, I could not say.

Now ask these same parents to consider a home in which the parents say to their newborn with great caring and concern, "Oh sweetie, we love you more than life itself. Welcome to the family. Now, we're going to sit down at the table and eat. You're welcome to watch. We hope you will. And, when you are older and can eat without spitting up, and can express some longing for and appreciation of the family meal, when you can distinguish it from a quick burger at McDonald's, we will, with deep joy, welcome you to join us here."

They will laugh, but they would never consider this is as a plan for home. Because children not only need to be fed, they need to be fed in the larger context of the family table. Children are fed in many ways. It is surely no accident that the distance from her mother's breast to her mother's face is the range at which a newborn's visual focus is most acute. Nourishment is about more than consuming calories.

Why do parents bring newborns to the table? I would ask you to consider all the tables of our common life as you ponder the question. She can't eat what everyone else is eating. He can't sit up in a chair. She can't take part in the conversation. He can't understand or articulate the concept of meal—and may never be able to do so. Parents bring their newborns to the table because the newborn is part of the family and the table is where the family gathers: To tell stories, to ask questions, to rejoice, to mourn, to talk, to listen, to rage, to return, to be remembered as family and to learn what it means to live in community. Every member of the family, whatever the age or intellectual ability, belongs there. The life is the preaching.

Parents must learn to recognize and respect the various ways children come to the table. The nursing newborn comes differently from the food-flinging toddler. The toddler comes differently from the babbling child. The child, who wants to tell you all about his day, comes differently from the sullen teenager, who, if my experience is any guide, will try to avoid coming at all. Is there a parent here whose teenager has not at one time or another risen from the table, screaming some bizarre variation on the Barney (the purple dinosaur) theme to the effect that "I hate you, you hate me, we're a dysfunctional family"?

So why do we welcome, and welcome again and again, our teenagers to the table? Why don't we follow their fit with one of our own, barring him from the table, throwing her chair in the alley, cutting off the corner of the table where he sits and serving only those who behave and who are grateful?

We welcome teenagers to the table for the same reason we first welcomed them as infants: They are part of the family, members of this community and the table is where this family, this community, gathers. It is that plain, that painful and that true. It is simple, though never easy: We are bound to one another and the table is the symbol both of our bond and of all the ways we strain against that bond. The table in my house is scratched and nicked and gouged. There are burn marks. The varnish is peeling. Not all of those who are welcome there are present now. Distance keeps some away; anger and resentment have kept us all away at one time or another. But the table remains, as do our places at it. Guests come and we all sit closer. There is room. The preaching is the life. And the preaching, as I have heard it from my own children, is not that we are some model family, "the liturgical Von Trapps," as one put it. The preaching is that there is a table, however scarred and however scarred those who gather around it may be. There is a table, with room for all who would come. That is the life and so it is the preaching.

For affirmation that the preaching is the life, we need to look no further than the Rite of Baptism for Children. The church speaks hard words to parents: "It will be your duty to teach her to keep God's commandments as Christ taught us." Then the church asks a question only new parents would be foolish enough to answer in the affirmative without fear and trembling: "Do you clearly understand what you are undertaking?" Listen to that. The church addresses the *parents* with these words. Why not the parish priest, the deacon or the catechists? Because it is the parents who are already doing the daily work of teaching the child. It is they who are feeding, rocking and singing to the child. It is they who are bringing the child to the table. They are teaching her, probably without ever using words, what it means to be part of a community. They are teaching him what it means to be a member of an order in Catholic homes—the order of the baptized. The child is one of the baptized all the time and everywhere, and at home she begins to learn what that means. If the parents are striving to be wise and loving, they are planting and nurturing within the child a heartfelt confidence, first in the beloved he can see—his parents—and then in the Beloved God he cannot see, but can only glimpse in our faces and through our deeds.

In the small community of the household, the parents are the ordinary ministers of the faith life of the home and of the formation of those in their care. They are the preachers of the word, for they are the livers of the life, the ones who model what it means to be human and to be baptized. And the ritual, as good rituals do, reveals truth, here, the truth that, "It will be your duty—the parent's duty—to bring him up to keep God's commandments as Christ taught us." The life is the preaching.

As Alexander Schmemann writes, before we can speak of humans as *homo sapiens,* we have to speak of them in their first and truest sense as *homo adorans.* Schmemann says, "The first, basic definition of man is that he is the priest. He stands in the center of the world and unifies it in his act of blessing God . . ." Before we can speak of man or woman, child or adult, lay or ordained, we have to speak of ourselves in the first and truest sense as the baptized, the priests, prophets and kings who are together church. Before we can speak of home as one reality or church as another, we have to speak of the font, the common womb of the assembly. To paraphrase Schmemann, the first, basic definition of the Christian is that he and she, we, are the baptized. And to be baptized is to become a member of an *ordo,* the order of the baptized.

As Andrew Ciferni teaches, to be a member of an order is to enter into a way of life. It is to answer the call to live a life congruent with the charism of the order. So for parents, it seems clear when and why children come to the family table. They come when they are born; they come because they are, from the beginning, full members of the community. Which is precisely what baptism means: to become a full member of the Christian community. It means plunging into the waters in which we all swim.

The difficulty comes when parents bring their baptized children from home to church. Because what they are learning about the order of the baptized around the table at home is quite different from what they learn about the order of the baptized around the table at church. In 1910 Pius X talked about the need for a child to distinguish between the family meal of the home and the sacred meal of the church as a sign of her readiness for communion. Putting aside the problem of emphasizing the differences between the tables rather than stressing the connections, I do not think what Pius X meant was that the child should learn, "The difference is that I am welcome at the table of the home and not welcome at the table of the church." It is curious that there is an emphasis on the differences in the sacrament of the table. Quite the opposite is true of infant baptism. Does anyone deliberately plunge an infant into icy water? Most priests and sacristans warm the water. I know it was my hope when each of my children was baptized that the baby would be reminded, in his flesh, along her skin, of every warm and soothing bath, from my womb to the tub at home to the welcoming womb of the church. The more the sacred nature of the meal at home reminds the child of the sacred meal at church, the better.

Still, we continue to emphasize the differences, and all the wrong ones at that. There are lessons being learned experientially, on the level young children learn, and one lesson is that the difference between the home table and the church table is that they are welcome at only one.

I invite you next Sunday to watch how the youngest of the baptized in our assemblies are treated. In my parish they are excommunicated. I use that term advisedly and deliberately, for that is the meaning of that "most severe ecclesiastical penalty," that it impedes one from receiving the sacraments. Watch as they are kept from the table to which their baptism bids them come. Joseph Bernardin wrote, "At this table we put aside every worldly separation based on culture [and] class. . . . Baptized, we no longer admit to distinctions based on age or sex or race or wealth." Don't we? Watch next Sunday as the community is silently divided into classes of the baptized—those who are welcome at the table by virtue, it would seem, of age and rational ability and those younger and pre-rational who are not. Pay attention to the story Max Johnson tells of the little boy who went with his parents in the communion procession. The minister of communion reached out to sign the young child with the cross on his forehead. The next Sunday, the child refused to accompany his parents in the procession. When they asked why, he pointed to the communion minister and said, "Because she x'ed me out." The life is the preaching.

Yet the altar table is the place where our baptism is made manifest, where we are made welcome at the generous feast provided by our gracious God. The altar table is where catechumens, the elect and young children can look around, listen and long. The altar table is where the neophytes, dripping wet from the Easter waters, are brought for their first glorious meal, there, to the table where they will be fed Sunday after Sunday on their long journey home to God.

We would not even entertain the thought of baptizing adults and then not welcoming them to the altar table. We would not consider first bringing adults into the order and then denying them the sustenance necessary for living the life of the order. Why do we baptize children if we will not then also bring them to the altar table? Is their baptism of a different kind? One Lord, one faith—many baptisms? Is it because infants lack understanding of what happens at the altar table, because they lack faith in the One they encounter there? But those same objections can be made to infant baptism itself, and it is our holy and ancient practice to baptize infants.

Indeed, a look at the structure of the Rite of Baptism for Children leads one to understand that neither faith (if by faith we mean "an intellectual conviction or set of beliefs") nor understanding is either expected or required of the infant brought forth for baptism.

The presider greets the *community* assembled to celebrate the baptism, not the child.

Then the presider begins a dialogue *with the parents and godparents,* the intent of which is to determine *their* desires and intentions. It is the *parents and godparents,* and not the child, who are questioned and placed under an obligation to lead the child into God. Adolf Adam writes that the rite of baptism

> takes seriously the fact that the one to be baptized is . . . an immature child. There is no artificial dialogue with a child that is still unable to speak; instead, the celebrant addresses the parents and godparents. He asks them about their profession of faith. True enough, he addresses the child at several points in the rite— the words of baptism, the anointing with chrism. There is, however, no pretense at a dialogue but simply words addressed to the child because the Church takes it seriously as a person.

But what if by faith we mean not "an intellectual conviction or set of beliefs," but, in the case of children, we accept Joseph Martos' definition of faith as "a heartfelt confidence in God and God's love," or Erik Erikson's definition of the touchstone of faith as "trust born of care"? What if the church would dare to learn something from the home, learn what parents already know, remember what they knew as children—that faith is something of which even the youngest child is capable. An infant who is fed when she is hungry, changed when she is wet and rocked when she is fussy will develop heartfelt confidence. Long before she can speak and long before she can define "confidence" or "faith."

As Mark Searle wrote, "the Christlike way of leaning into life is not necessarily anything which has to wait our conscious decision or deliberate choice. It is rather something which we discover to be already operative in us by the grace of God by the time we become aware of it." Like walking. We walk and skip and leap and run for years before we become aware of the mechanics or the miracles involved.

And if we can accept this truth about infant baptism, does it not follow that we can accept it about infant communion as well? If it is true, as Mark Searle's own son once said to him, "At home I'm your son, but at church I'm your brother," then how can we continue to treat our baptized children as neither sons nor daughters, brothers or sisters, but as strangers, those who have no place at the table?

Is this an argument against formation? No. To the contrary, it is an argument in favor of formation. Formation at home and at church, throughout all of life. But this is formation of learning from the wisdom of the home, formation remembering what parents already know; formation from the inside out and not the outside in; formation at the table, within the community; formation that respects the developmental stages of growth; formation knowing oneself—*before* one can even conceptualize or articulate self-knowledge, indeed, *whether* one can ever conceptualize or articulate self-knowledge—formation knowing oneself to be a full member of the life.

Why is it that child development researchers and teachers speak with such conviction of the importance of the first three years of life? Because the development there, beginning with the first single cell of life in the womb, is from the inside out and the effects of that development are irreversible. What is the lasting effect of keeping infants and young children from the table?

The psychologist Jerome Bruner writes that a person learns first by enacting, that is by standing in the action as a part of the action, and only then by imaging, and much later still by that abstract activity we call thinking. Consider: What is the first enacting that a child ever does? It is interesting that we are talking about tables and about communion—the eating and drinking of the baptized in holy union with God and one another—because the first enacting, the first way of knowing the world is through the human breast, that is, orally.

A healthy newborn, who can make no purposeful gestures, can suck and will go immediately after birth to do so at her mother's breast. Watch a baby: Everything, goes into the mouth. Hand him a toy and he will put it in his mouth. Give her your finger and she will suck on it. The first way any child knows is through tasting. The first way a child knows goodness, kindness, mercy, comfort, beauty and the deep pleasure of human touch is through the mouth, at the breast. Jesus, who comes to us in bread broken open and wine poured out, first knew the earth he redeemed through his mother's breast. "Oh, taste and see that the Lord is good," might be the hymn of praise of the loved and nourished child.

Children learn first in their bodies; parents know this. How do we teach children to speak, to sing, to walk, to pray? We speak with them, sing with them, walk with them, pray with them. Children learn in their bodies. Yet at church we continue to insist that they learn initially in their intellects: class first, then communion. The bar to receiving the sacrament is the child's inability to perform certain tasks, namely, to understand the rite on some intellectual level and to be able to articulate certain truths about the rite. Then the tone of first communion preparation has about it the feel of skills-testing and performance. The underlying questions are these: What are the things the child is supposed to learn in order to be admitted to this sacrament? What is the body of knowledge to be mastered? But that is precisely *not* how children learn, at least not until late childhood or early adolescence. And if that is the model, one of skills-testing and performance which requires a certain level of competence and volition, then the question must be asked: Why do we do all this at age seven, when children are still too young for the abstract thinking the model demands? If that is the model, the larger and more important question remains: Why do we baptize infants at all?

Think for a moment about the inside out formation of family life, a formation that begins before the child's skills, abilities or even her personality, have been made known to the parents; before any sort of testing is possible. Of course, there are parents who have instituted skill-testing for their children: I am reminded of the prospective adoptive couple who placed an ad looking for a pregnant Ivy League coed with an SAT score above 1400 and well above-average height. All of us instinctively know that such an approach to parenthood is frighteningly misguided.

We understand that the commitment parents rightly make to their newborns is similar to the commitment God makes to us in baptism: open-ended, not hedged round with guarantees. God pledges to be with the baptized, even when the baptized abandon God. It is about God's goodness and is not dependent on the consistent moral skills of the one to be baptized. In any skills test for baptism we would fail.

Melissa Musick Nussbaum

At home we do not say: "You must learn, accomplish, explain or perform in order to be welcomed to the family table." We say "Welcome to the family table, little one, whose character and personality is yet to reveal itself. Welcome to the table—and now begins the lifelong formation of learning how to gather here, to listen here and to be heard here." Now begins the roughly 20 years of "elbows off the table" and "fingers out of the nose" and "chew with your mouth closed" and "don't make vomiting noises when your sister sits down beside you." That is formation at the table, formation from the inside out. Because the life is the preaching.

The question before us is how the table of the home is reflected in the altar table of the church: Where do the two tables meet? For infants and young children there is no real meeting. The home table simply is not reflected in the altar table. They have been welcomed at one since before they had memory. They are turned away from the other while all around them, mothers, fathers, brothers and sisters are fed.

It is said that the strongest ritual gesture is transcultural. What stronger gesture could there be than to take a single loaf of bread, break it into many pieces and then share it with some, but not all? Even a two-year old can comprehend what is happening in that moment. And it is happening at the precise moment in her development when she most wants to mimic the adults around her. Just consider that for a moment, the folly of our putting off "full initiation" to the time in a child's life when she is least interested in either following the example of the adults around her or of needing their advice. We ask teenagers to make a mature commitment to their faith (after having them paint the rectory, of course) at the time when most of them entertain strong "Party of Five" fantasies. ("Party of Five" is a television show wherein five kids are left to fend for themselves after their parents thoughtfully took out adequate life insurance and then died. Quickly. And together.) But of course the confusion is deep here, too, because we call confirmation a sacrament of maturity. But just let two recently confirmed announce their intention to marry or get a tatoo or start a record label called "Craptacular Records," as a young man of my acquaintance did, and watch the reaction of adults. Just let one ask to be a communion minister or a lector and see the reaction to that. But during those very early years there is hardly a parent who has not heard the cry of a young child at communion, "I want some of that." Or, "I want to do what you're doing"— which, incidentally and after all, is the basis of all human formation.

A woman once came up to me and promised to send me a picture taken at her older daughter's first communion at St. Michael's in Bedford, Texas, during the Easter season of 1990. What makes her weep every time she looks at it, the woman told me, is the sight of her younger daughter's outstretched hands as she too comes forward, a baptized Christian to the table of the baptized, asking for what is already hers, asking to be fed.

She told me, "I showed our pastor this picture. He said, 'Hmmm.' I shared it with our youth minister, a mother of four. She said, 'Ahhh, she wants some, too.'"

And she concluded, "Those who have eyes to see . . ."

Last October I visited my daughter Elisabeth, who was interning with Frontier Nursing Service in Hyden, Kentucky. Every Friday night, Elisabeth went to Alabam Morgan's house to learn to quilt, and Alabam would invite her to church on Sunday, to the Hurt's Creek Church of Christ. On the Sunday morning I was there, Elisabeth and I went to church with Alabam as her guests. It came time for communion and a layman rose from the assembly and asked all who would to come to the table.

After a time, when it seemed that communion was drawing to a close, he stood again and looked out and asked, quietly and simply, "Has everybody been fed? Are there any in need?" And, taking the cup and the plate, he went out to some who had been overlooked and served them.

I am so grateful to have witnessed such hospitality and to have heard spoken in that church the question I raise now: "Has everybody been fed? Are there any in need?" And I bring this charge. Let us take up the bread and the wine, the Body and Blood of our Lord Jesus Christ, and go out to those who have not been fed, to those who are still in need, so that the table of the home and the table of the church might be reflections, one of the other, welcome tables for all the baptized, no matter how young or how weak or how easily overlooked.

Richard S. Vosko

God's House Is
Our House, Too.

Who or what expresses and communicates the identity of the church? An answer to my question may be found in the title of a recent article by Nathan Mitchell—"Ritual's Job: To Tell Us Who and Why We Are."[1] It is the job of ritual to express our self-identity, to let us know who and why we are.

Generally, the liturgical movement in North America has fared well. Building on the marvelous foundations of the 1940s—the Liturgical Conference and the Liturgical Arts Society—and the recent letters by pastors such as Cardinal Roger Mahony[2] and Archbishop Rembert Weakland,[3] we have succeeded in using our resources and talents to build up the church and its liturgy. The emergence of varied liturgical ministries, the resurgence of the catechumenate, the composition of new pieces of music for use in the liturgy, the increased interest in scripture study and some evidence of more accessible, intelligible homilies are indicators of this growth.

Some struggles do persist. We meet obstacles when working with issues of language. We search for ways to balance popular piety and public liturgy. We strive for more inclusion in our rituals. We misunderstand what it means to say that the church is a primary symbol at the eucharistic liturgy.

The environment for worship is another area of church life that still needs our attention. If it is the job of ritual to tell us who and why we are, do our worship spaces reflect our self-understanding? Or, do our churches, whether new or renovated, hinder the growth and practice of the church's liturgy?

In this article I will present an outline of three themes that are useful in evaluating the environment needed for Catholic worship. The first theme deals with the nature of the church, "Who is the church?" The second deals with the way the church prays, "How does the church pray?" I begin with an outline of these very familiar topics in order to establish a foundation for thinking about the environment for worship. These starting points are key ones because so many churches are being built or renovated without any consideration given to ecclesiology or liturgy. I will then discuss the third theme, "Where does the church pray?"

Who Is the church?

In order to understand the significance of the postconciliar liturgical movement, it is essential to understand who the church is and what that church does. Ecclesiology and liturgy are siblings in this regard. That is why many of the provocative liturgical questions that arise today will probably not have liturgical answers. The solutions will be ecclesiological ones. The ways in which the church teaches, makes decisions and worships are based in ecclesiology, in the answer to the question, "Who is the church?"

The Second Vatican Council heralded a universal call to holiness to all baptized persons and thereby formally invited clergy and laity alike to share their gifts and work together to fulfill the mission of the church.[4] One major responsibility of the church is to work for peace and justice. Jesus lovingly identified with people who were estranged, oppressed and poor, and gave them hope. We must identify with this and take responsibility for acting as Jesus did if we are truly to see the paschal mystery as our own. Our life as a community of faith is bound up with our responsibility to establish peace and justice. Our liturgical environments have to embody this fact. The songs we sing, the prayers we say, the homilies we experience, the art we create and the buildings we design—all must assist us in making connections with the social responsibilities of the church. For example, some (if not all) of the art in our churches should prompt a desire to address the social injustice that exists in our communities. The purpose of the church building is not to help us get away from issues of peace and justice anymore than the purpose of the liturgy is to view the world through rose-colored glasses.

Another primary responsibility of the church is the celebration of the paschal mystery. Our embrace of the paschal mystery is made possible through our ritual acts. Our celebration of the paschal mystery affirms who we are as the Mystical Body of Christ, proclaims what we believe and nourishes us to carry out the gospel mission. The Mass not only *belongs* to the entire church; it is precisely *about* the church—the Mystical Body of Christ. The liturgy of the eucharist is not about something outside of us nor is it about watching something done for us. Saint Augustine states: "If you are the body of Christ and his members, you are the sacrament of what is placed on the table of the Lord; it is the sacrament of what you are when you receive" (Sermon 272).

Every effort must be made to commemorate the paschal mystery in a most inspiring and reverent manner. The careful selection and use of words, songs, gestures, movements, artworks, smells, textures and objects in our rites, along with a deliberate use of space, light and sounds, draws the assembled community deeper into the mystery being memorialized.

The celebration of the paschal mystery, and the responsibility to work for peace and justice that is connected to it, are entrusted to the whole church and not just select members. The question is, when the church celebrates the paschal mystery how well does its place of worship reflect this understanding of who the church is and what the church does?

How Does the Church Pray?

Some Catholics say they can get just as much out of the liturgy by not participating in an active and conscious way. So they withdraw from the group. They recite their own prayers and avoid seating plans that promote interaction. This is not the behavior one would expect from someone who has been invited by God to share in the eucharistic mystery.

Even though religion is a very personal spiritual cradle for most people, the act of public worship cannot, by its very nature, be private.[5] It is not another popular devotion nor is it the time for enacting one's private devotions. The penchant for such a passive attitude during the liturgy is not difficult to understand when we consider that for a long time Catholics have been taught to be docile, reverent and completely quiet while the priest said his Mass. The responsibility here lies with pastoral educators. More effort should be made to help adult Catholics understand that it is their responsibility to participate actively and consciously in the paschal celebration.[6] In his apostolic letter *Dies Domini,* Pope John Paul II reminds us that "the faithful must realize that, because of the common priesthood received in baptism, 'they participate in the offering of the Eucharist.'"[7]

There are other compelling reasons for helping Catholics learn how to engage in the art of ritual making. I will briefly cite two references. Anthropologist Theodore Jennings wrote that ritual activity is a way of gaining knowledge. To an observer who is invited to see, approve, understand or recognize the ritual action, the display transmits an understanding of the ritual and its participants. He continues:

> Ritual knowledge is gained not by detached observation or contemplation but through action. It is in and through the action (gesture, step, etc.) that ritual knowledge is gained, not in advance of it, nor after it. If ritual knowledge were prior to the action then we would be reduced once again to understanding the ritual as an illustration or demonstration of what is already known in some other way.[8]

Catholics who think that attendance at Mass is a time to receive what is distributed to them by others or a time to fulfill an obligation without regard to what is happening in the room, have not yet dis-covered or accepted their responsibility to participate fully in the rite, or, one could say, the paschal mystery. Perhaps they have not learned that the celebration or the memorialization of the paschal mystery may *depend* on their participation. As Mary Collins comments, that which is "efficacious for real eucharistic presence comprises the ritual symbolic process, *doing and saying,* by which the body of bodies that gathers in the local church brings itself into being as the Body of Christ by the power of the Holy Spirit alive in the assembly."[9]

Where Does the Church Pray?

If we believe that the church is the mystical body of Christ, and that the liturgy is something that belongs to and is enacted by that body, then there is a compelling reason to define where the church prays.

A great number of chapels, churches and cathedrals still have not been reordered to accommodate the reformed rites of the church. To continue to avoid this task is tantamount to saying the spatial arrangement does not matter or that the role of the assembly is not that important. Consequently, many communities gather and arrange themselves for worship in settings that resemble lecture halls, complete with a stage and an area for an audience. But as Aidan Kavanagh once remarked: "Communities do not cohere around lecture halls. But everyone loves a parade!"[10]

Even in many new churches one can find settings that promote separation between members of the assembly, effectively creating two groups: spectators and actors. Just draw an imaginary line in front of the altar in most churches and see what percentage of members of the assembly are still seated on one side of the table. Some fan-shaped or semicircular arrangements continue to foster a "delivery system" approach to the sacraments. Michael Kwatera, OSB, wrote recently:

> It is sad to hear that some still see the church building as divided into "clerical space" and "lay space" rather than as a unified sacred space that is made so by the sacred people of God (both ordained and non-ordained) and their sacred actions in company with Christ. One must rejoice in those who know that whereas

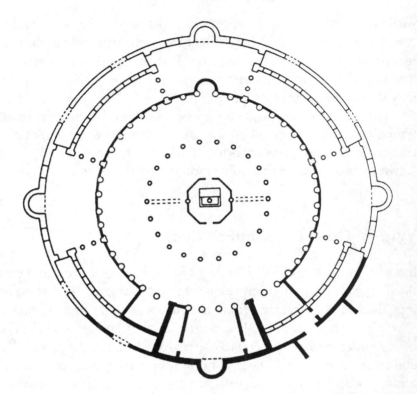

Santo Stefano Rotundo (by Pope Saint Simplicius, 468-483).
Taken from *Churches of Rome* by Pierre Grimal
(The Vendome Press, NY, 1997), 42.

the provisions for seating "must express a hierarchical arrangement and the diversity of offices, they should at the same time
form a complete and organic unity, clearly expressive of the
unity of the entire holy people" (*General Instruction of the
Roman Missal*, 257).[11]

Perhaps the fault is ours. Since the Council we have focused on
the placement of four items: font, altar, ambo, chair. Unfortunately, in
many churches all of these furnishings have been placed on a single
large platform in front of the congregation while very little has been
done to encourage the members of the assembly to gather around
them. The concentration on these four items has led to the development of rather static places for worship and therefore liturgical
celebrations that are not uplifting or prayerful. Floor plans should be

designed to create a more inclusive worship setting, one that honors the different offices and ministries in the church without relegating the members of the assembly to spaces that encourage or demand their passivity.

The problem is not resolved by creating spaces that appear "heavenly" or "transcendent" or "mysterious." These are terms used by some Catholics to describe what they feel is missing in contemporary places of worship, but these words have more to do with decorative styles and matters of taste. The much larger issue has to do with designing buildings that will draw the faithful deeper into their own mystery that is revealed in the unfolding ritual drama of the liturgy. To do this, the assembly must be honored as a player, not seen as a spectator.

Oddly, many people believe that an ornate worship setting is a normal part of the Catholic tradition. Still others claim that only certain architectural styles can provide appropriate settings for the celebration of the Mass. Such positions show little consideration for the diversity that exists within the Catholic tradition, not to mention the history of Christian church architecture. The literature is not convincing enough to suggest that a space more decorated or a specific architectural style is what will create a better experience of the holy or of the New Jerusalem. After all, we do not wait in joyful hope for yet another *place*. What we do have are great expectations for a fuller *experience* of the presence of God in our lives on this planet a well as forever more. That is why the responsibilities mentioned earlier in this article are essential to the life of the church. The hopeful members of the church are those who can generate an experience of the holy that can inspire others. The manner in which the liturgy is enacted will serve as the ultimate touchstone for this experience. The space must serve that liturgy. The liturgical event or the people engaged in the mystery should never be a slave to the space. Frits van der Meer wrote:

> For far too long our sensibility has been the prisoner of those charming little lateral chapels; it has lost itself among all those secondary figures, among that crowded gallery of Gothic, flamboyant and baroque "commentaries." In our world today, it is a communal home which is demanded for the people of God. Also

demanded is an inspired and coherent liturgy offered with almost perfect drastic clarity.[12]

There does not seem to be anything meritorious or authentic about designing a new church building that is a replica of a religious building from another era or another country. Creating such imitations is what Disney World and Las Vegas do very well. Walking through make-believe versions of the *Arc de Triomphe* (not in Paris, France, but in Las Vegas) or the Hall of Prayer for Good Harvests in the Temple of Heaven (not in Beijing, China, but in the Epcot Center) can provide an entertaining experience. However, these structures are simply not authentic. There is little reason to think, short of shear sentimentality, that the replication of religious architectural styles or interiors from another age will serve worshiping communities with an authentic experience of the sacred or holy. It is as if the transferal of relics from a bygone time will automatically transform the people of God today. Houses of prayer are not museums. What is required instead is an architectural setting that says the entire gathered assembly is invited to full engagement in the rites. A.W. N. Pugin wrote:

> The great test of architectural beauty is the fitness of the design to the purpose for which it is intended and that the style of the building should so correspond with its use that the spectator may at once perceive the purpose for which it was intended.[13]

What should be done with a good, older church building—built by ancestors and still used for worship today? Keeping it stable is the first responsibility. Respecting the artwork is the second. Evaluating how well it functions for worship today is the third. Good liturgical design direction from a trained professional and a good dose of imagination can help to transform almost any well-adorned, older church building into a place of public ritual without taking away its innate beauty and architectural integrity.

What kind of space will honor the work of the assembly as it celebrates the paschal event of Jesus Christ? First, it must be a space that is not just a container for ritual furnishings, liturgical appointments and adornments. Second, a church building must be the embodiment of the people of God. A review of the language used in

Richard S. Vosko

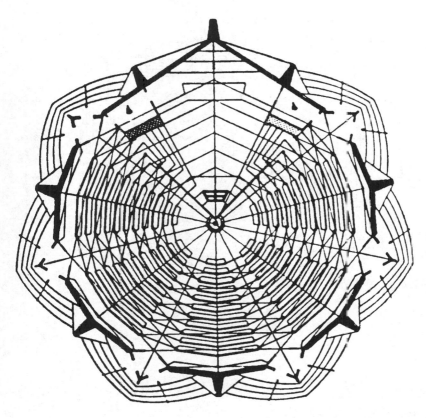

Sternkirche (by Otto Bartning, 1922).
Taken from *Architecture for Worship*, Edward A. Sövik
(Augsburg Publishing, Minneapolis MN, 1973), 30.

Dedication of a Church and an Altar clearly reveals that the building is a metaphor for the church—the mystical body of Christ. Third, the space should foster a high degree of participation in the rituals.

Designs for worship environments should be based on the desire to promote the engagement of the entire assembly, not just a few liturgical ministers. To achieve this, more attention will have to be given to how the assembly behaves during worship. How, when and where its members sit, stand, kneel, process, see, hear, touch, smell, etc., must be taken into consideration when planning a space for worship. The perception that everything important can be done only by someone else must be clarified. We must challenge the notion that one must only see and hear in order to participate. Liturgy is more

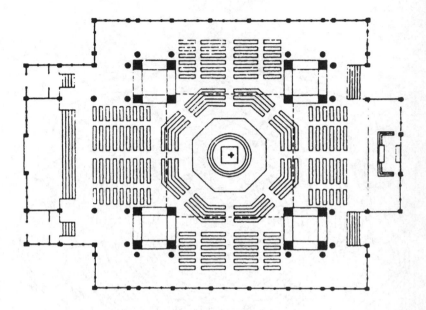

St. Joseph Church, Le Havre (by Auguste Perret, 1959).
Taken from *The New Churches of Europe*, G. E. Kidder Smith
(Holt, Rinehart & Winston, NY, 1964), 106.

like a rhythmic dance and less like a lecture. The experience of worship should convey that all the members of the body of Christ are engaged together in the celebration of the paschal mystery. It seems to me that a worship space organized around a central axis can do this very well. Aside from the obvious symbolism of a circle, which makes it a logical shape in which to celebrate our sacrament of unity, there are other reasons that a centralized plan is an appropriate one for worship environments.

Research in the field of proxemics (the study of the nature of the spatial separations that people maintain and the relation of this separation to environment)[14] can give us new insights on seating plans for the assembly. This research can help us discern which seating arrangements can foster more participation in the assembly during worship. For example, a distinction can be made between *sociofugal* and *sociopetal* settings.[15] A sociofugal seating pattern, with straight rows of seats all facing in one direction, discourages interaction among the participants. A sociopetal seating pattern, with seats arranged in a circular pattern, encourages more interaction and engagement. Put simply, if you want to achieve more active, conscious participation during liturgy, the sociofugal seating plan would not be the best choice.

Practical considerations also come into play here. In a church that seats 1,000 people in long, straight rows facing one direction, the last row of seats can be 120 feet or more away from the altar. In a more circular seating arrangement of 1,000 seats, no person is more than 60 feet away from the altar table.[16] Proximity to the action of the liturgy can encourage greater participation.

Because the church building should serve the needs of various liturgies, the overall organization of the worship space could be polycentric without being confusing. In a polycentric church building there would be ceremonial centers for washing, reading, eating and drinking, or just sitting still. This would help individuals and the assembly as a whole move through the space in a rhythmic, graceful, prayerful, song-filled manner. These centers would actually comprise a holistic and unified worship arena for the gathered assembly. The entire space would be a centralized one.

The centralized plan is not new to the Catholic tradition. See the floor plans included with this article for examples. Edward Sövik's thoughts on Otto Bartning's *Sternkirche* summarize the intent of the centralize plan.

> Otto Bartning had proposed earlier that the long and narrow processional or axial plans of traditional buildings are inappropriate to Christian understanding. The proper view of the gathered congregation, he said, is that of a cohesive community of clergy and laymen whose members should be aware of their unity as the body of Christ, the family of God, the household of believers. When they meet it is not as individuals at prayer and not as a congregation of observers in attendance at a clerical ritual, but as a community acting together.[17]

Otto Bartning saw the circular room as the proper reflection of the understanding of the church as the body of Christ. Such a shape not only symbolizes unity and coherence but effectively encourages it.[18] I propose that such a plan can once again serve the church. It

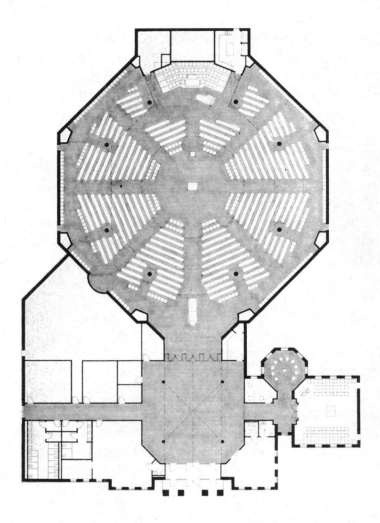

St. John the Evangelist, West Chester OH
(by John Ruetschle Associates, with liturgical
design consultant Richard S. Vosko, 1999).

Richard S. Vosko

can eliminate both physical and psychological barriers between the ministers and the members of the assembly. It can reduce the distance between the assembly and the ritual, as well as between members of the assembly themselves. It can help the assembly focus on the ritual actions, which will foster more active, conscious participation in the liturgy. It can provide a spiritual commentary for the Christian pilgrimage similar to that generated by the mandala. It can proclaim that the gathered church is presiding over its own mystery.

Worshiping in a space that is organized around a centralized plan requires imagination and some risks. We have referred to our churches as "God's house" probably from the time that Tertullian coined the expression in the early Third Century. Harmless as it may seem, calling our places of worship a domicile for God has unwittingly affected our understanding of the primary purpose of a house for the church. To call a place of worship "God's house" could conjure up romantic notions of where one can find God. However, it can also obscure the significant differences between a religious building designed to house the worship of the church and temples that are designed to house the deity. That is why God's house has to be our house, too.

God's House Is Our House, Too

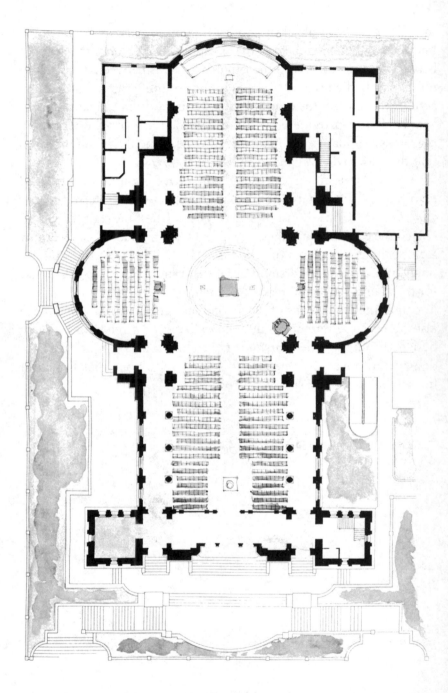

St. James Cathedral, Seattle WA (by Bumgardner Architects
with liturgical design consultant Richard S. Vosko, 1999).

1. In *Ministry & Liturgy* 26 (June–July 1999), 6.

2. *Gather Faithfully Together* (Chicago: Liturgy Training Publications, 1997).

3. *A Church Without Walls* (Milwaukee: Archdiocese of Milwaukee, 1999).

4. Vatican II, dogmatic constitution *Lumen gentium* (On the Church) (November 21, 1964), 37–41.

5. Vatican II, constitution *Sacrosanctum Concilium* (On the Sacred Liturgy) (SC) (December 4, 1963), 26.

6. SC, 14.

7. Art. 51.

8. Theodore W. Jennings, Jr., "On Ritual Knowledge" in Ronald L. Grimes, ed., *Readings in Ritual Studies* (Englewood Cliffs NJ: Prentice Hall, 1996).

9. Mary Collins, "The Church and the Eucharist" in Judith A. Dwyer, ed., *Proceedings of the Fifth-second Annual Convention, Catholic Theological Society of America* (Jamaica NY: St. John's University, 1997), 26.

10. From my notes taken in an early morning class with Aidan Kavanagh at the University of Notre Dame, Summer, 1972.

11. "A Chosen Race, Royal Priesthood, Holy People: A Place for Us" in *Assembly* 25 (March 1999), 12–13.

12. *Keerpunt der Middeleeuwen* (1950), 160ff, from Frédéric Debuyst, *Modern Architecture and Christian Celebration,* Ecumenical Studies in Worship, no. 18 (Richmond VA: John Knox Press, 1968), 29.

13. "Contrasts; or a Parallel between the Noble Edifices of the Fourteenth and Fifteenth Centuries and Similar Building of the Present Day; Shewing the Present Decay of Taste," (Salisbury, 1836), from Heathcote and Spens, *Church Builders* (West Sussex: John Wiley & Sons 1997), 9.

14. See E. T. Hall, *Handbook for Proxemic Research* (Washington, D.C.: Society for the Anthropology of Visual Research) and R. Sommers. *Personal Space* (Englewood Cliffs NJ: Prentice Hall, 1969), to mention only two such works.

15. See H. Osmond, "The Relationship Between Architect and Psychiatrist," in C. Goshen, ed., *Psychiatric Architecture* (Washington, D.C.: American Psychiatric Association, 1959).

16. See my "Where We Learn Shapes Our Learning," in R. Hienstra, ed., *Creating Environments for Effective Adult Learning* (San Francisco: Jossey-Bass, 1991).

17. *Architecture for Worship* (Minneapolis: Augsburg, 1973).

18. Ibid.

Other Books in This Series

The major presentations from past annual conferences of the Notre Dame Center for Pastoral Liturgy are available from LTP as the following publications:

Children in the Assembly of the Church (1991). Five addresses that explore the place of children in the liturgy, the contribution they make and the need to celebrate the liturgy well with children.

The Renewal that Awaits Us (1995). Presentations on the renewals already undertaken in the liturgy and considerations of what still needs to be pursued.

Traditions and Transitions (1996). Reflections on the dynamic of ambiguities and changes in the decades of transition following Vatican II.

The Changing Face of the Church (1997). A collection of papers that seeks to understand how the many different cultures of the people of the church influence the liturgies we celebrate.

The Many Presences of Christ (1998). Essays that explore the meaning of Christ's presences in the gathered assembly, the proclaimed word, the sacraments, the minister and the consecrated bread and wine.